Costa del Crime

Costa del Crime

WENSLEY CLARKSON

JOHN BLAKE

Published by John Blake Publishing Ltd,
3 Bramber Court, 2 Bramber Road,
London W14 9PB, England

www.blake.co.uk

First published in paperback in 2006

ISBN 978 1 84454 257 4

British Library Cataloguing-in-Publication Data:

A catalogue record for this book is available from the British Library.

Design by www.envydesign.co.uk

Printed in the UK by CPI Bookmarque, Croydon, CR0 4TD

5 7 9 10 8 6 4

Papers used by John Blake Publishing are natural, recyclable products made
from wood grown in sustainable forests. The manufacturing processes
conform to the environmental regulations of the country of origin.

All photographs from the author's collection, except p19, p29 © Press
Association/Empics; p135 © Photo News; p265, p275 © Rex Features

To the good – and bad – residents of Southern Spain
I encountered while writing this book

Crime leaves a trail like a water beetle;
Like a snail, it leaves its shine;
Like a horse-mango, it leaves its reek.

OLD SPANISH PROVERB

CONTENTS

AUTHORS NOTE

Many of the characters featured here would not have made it into this book if it had not been for my numerous contacts on the Costa del Sol. Many of them, naturally, would rather you did not know their identity. So to all the faces I've encountered, and to all the ordinary, law-abiding folk from southern Spain who've also helped me, I say thank you. Without you, this book would not have been possible.

Most of the dialogue used here was drawn from actual interviews. Some was reconstructed from available documents; a few descriptions were reconstituted from the memory of others. There are no hidden agendas in these stories, and I make no apology for the explicit sexual action and strong language.

On a number of occasions throughout the book, I have changed certain names. This has been done to protect both the innocent and the guilty.

Wensley Clarkson
Costa del Sol, 2006

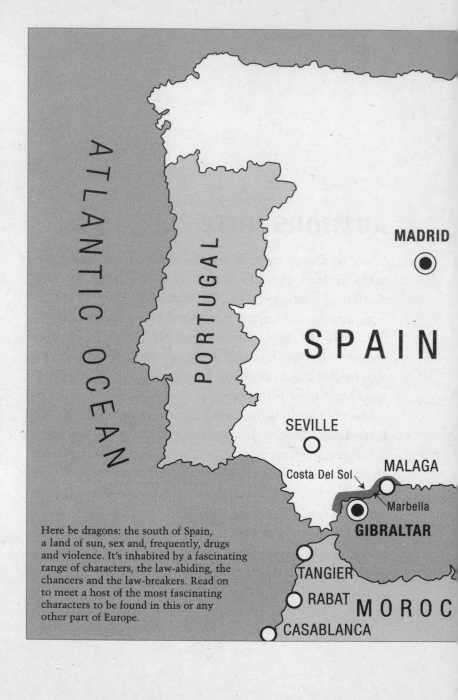

ATLANTIC OCEAN

PORTUGAL

SPAIN

MADRID

SEVILLE

Costa Del Sol

MALAGA

Marbella

GIBRALTAR

TANGIER

RABAT

MOROC

CASABLANCA

Here be dragons: the south of Spain, a land of sun, sex and, frequently, drugs and violence. It's inhabited by a fascinating range of characters, the law-abiding, the chancers and the law-breakers. Read on to meet a host of the most fascinating characters to be found in this or any other part of Europe.

INTRODUCTION

The average daily temperature on Spain's Costa del Sol is 20 degrees centigrade, with at least 320 days of sunshine every year. Thanks to this wonderful climate, the gentle slopes and fertile plains that once rose up from the beaches of the Costa del Sol have been transformed into concrete jungles of hotels and high-rise apartments. Those who discovered seaside villages like Torremolinos and Estepona more than 30 years ago have watched in horror as the area has become overrun by tourists and foreign residents. And there seems little chance of it slowing down.

With more than 60 miles of beaches, including picturesque coves and vast overhanging cliffs, the area behind the shoreline used to feature acres of olive and fruit groves and sweeping pine-covered hills. But all that has been replaced by vast urbanisations of detached housing occupied by the Costa del Sol's richer residents who have moved back towards the mountains to try and escape the 'lowlifes' by the sea.

East from Estepona is a typical example: San Pedro, once a sleepy fishing village, is now dominated by bland concrete buildings and dual carriageways. Its attractive whitewashed houses, adorned with geraniums and jasmine in window boxes, used to provide a picture-postcard backdrop. They are now long gone.

Marbella remains a bustling seaside town with hundreds of bars and cafés. Old Marbella includes a Mudejar-style Church of La Encarnacion; marvellous buildings of Moorish design now serve as municipal centres. Travelling inland from Marbella is an area which was once the last Moorish stronghold on the Iberian Peninsula. This mountainous region features dozens of tiny villages, some up as high as 4,000 feet. But the Brits and other foreigners have already invaded these ancient communities by building characterless housing estates on any available land.

Back on the coast, the yacht marina down at Fuengirola contains some of the tackiest vessels afloat. Unattractive bars named after British pubs litter the area. A couple of miles further east on the coast is Torremolinos, first built up in the 1960s as a luxury holiday location by Spanish dictator Franco, and now in need of a lot more than a good lick of paint. Goodness knows what the Romans and Arabs who settled in the area almost a thousand years ago would have made of it all. Phoenician necropolises still stand in some towns, as do the remains of Roman aqueducts; but the area's history tends to be ignored by most of the Brits who have arrived in their droves since the 1960s.

In the bright sunshine of the modern-day Costa del Sol it is sometimes difficult to appreciate that this entire area has been developed in less than half a lifetime. Sleepy coves with crystal-clear water have been replaced by overcrowded beach bars featuring spivs, drug dealers and sexual predators; there is a constant noise of people and cars at all times of the day and night. No wonder the pace of life here is frenetic and local people are suspicious and unfriendly until they know precisely what it is you want.

Although the provincial government of Malaga is keen to continue encouraging tourists with open arms, it is also anxious to stem the tide of criminality so that in the long term this once beautiful area does not lose its appeal as a genuine holiday destination. But it is difficult to get away from the facts. Dotting the coastline used to be ancient stone towers and fortresses, which served as lookout posts during the Arab occupation of this part of Spain. These days the police are more likely to be watching for drugs smugglers and illegal immigrants. Marbella itself has become the unofficial capital of the Costa del Crime.

Few people realise that the murder rate in this part of Spain has risen by 70 per cent over the past 15 years. Crime itself is said to have doubled. Drug-related killings between gangsters are virtually a weekly occurrence. Clashes between British, Spanish, Eastern

European and Russian villains are commonplace. They run 'businesses' ranging from brothels to live internet sex services, from boat and property companies to satellite-TV installation firms; and then of course there are the obligatory multi-million-pound drug deals.

Crime is the Costa del Sol's second-biggest industry after tourism. It's not an easy statistic to handle, is it? Tony Blair's Britain has seen a gold-rush to this area; and when British gangsters spend their millions, they help keep legitimate businesses afloat, especially in the thriving coastal resorts. When Spain tightened up its extradition laws in 1987, the commonly held belief was that all the big-name villains would find themselves without a bolthole and be sent home to the UK. But because the change in the law was not retrospective, many British criminals simply based themselves full time in southern Spain and became even more involved in illegal enterprises. As one old-time crook said, 'All that publicity about how the Spaniards had cracked down on us really took the heat off many of the big names down here and helped them thrive, because the reality was that the Spanish police were much easier to handle than the cops back home. And most of the characters out here haven't broken any laws back in Britain for many years, so what can they be extradited for?'

Headlines insisting that the glory days of the Costa del Crime are over are very wide of the mark. Back in 2001, the Home Secretary Jack Straw joined forces with his Spanish counterpart and claimed that, under new extradition rules, these British criminals in Spain could be brought back to the UK to face justice.

Despite signing a treaty with Spain back in 1985, the procedures remain complex and time consuming. A villain with a skilful lawyer can still drag out the procedure for months, and sometimes even years. It took nine months to extradite M25 killer and master criminal Kenneth Noye, despite this new spirit of co-operation.

These days, few of the numerous British villains on the Costa del Crime are on the run from justice. They pose as businessmen and earn fortunes while the Spanish authorities are either powerless to prosecute or, in some cases, simply turn a blind eye. Local police often take the attitude that, because the drug shipments never stay in Spain for long and most of the violence is between criminals, it's not worth their while trying to arrest many of these characters. Incalculable fortunes, rather than sun, sea and sand, is now the allure of the Costa del Crime.

Many criminals have even retired after making their fortunes ferrying hash and cocaine across Europe. Others point to the number of cranes on the horizon in resorts like San Pedro and Puerto Banus as the ultimate proof that business is still booming. Most of the criminals operating out here don't even speak basic Spanish, but they let their money do the talking for them. Even when some do get arrested they know there are many ways to avoid jail. As one old-timer says, 'The trick is to get bail. About €15,000 normally does it. And once you're out, you're out for ever.

New name, new apartment – and the world's your oyster once again.'

Many of these characters look utterly ordinary, like any of the overwhelmingly blameless Brits who live or holiday on the Costa del Sol. And these people get respect from many ordinary people because their criminal activities carry little or no stigma whatsoever. Tucked away in the hills, behind all the most popular Costa del Crime resorts, are countless such villains enjoying a view of the Mediterranean, a decent pension and moaning about how the young hoods are giving the coast a bad reputation.

The police are virtually powerless to do anything because, under Spanish law, conspiracy does not exist as a crime. Even the most mountainous pile of incriminating and circumstantial evidence is useless unless the suspect is caught red-handed – sitting on top of a shipment of drugs or carrying a smoking gun.

But all this goes a long way to explaining how so many of the tens of thousands of bars and restaurants and timeshare complexes on the Costa del Crime stay afloat in the face of fierce competition. Some are laundering money so much that traditional profit is almost irrelevant.

One Spanish property expert recently described the construction activity in places like Marbella and Estepona as 'astounding'. The number of permits for housing and corporate units has almost doubled in the last ten years. There is currently close to £1 billion worth of business going on. Seventy-five per cent of that money is laundered from the proceeds of crime. Where else do these people get their money?

The Costa del Crime has become a vast building site with drugs money financing housing, shopping and corporate developments that will generate clean, hard euros. Those who reckon criminal activity along the sunlit stretch is exclusively the domain of small-time crooks on the run could not be more wrong.

Ever-diminishing Spanish police recruitment has led to officers being diverted from the usual criminal activities such as prostitution and drugs, allowing them to thrive. Statistics from the Costa del Sol make worrying reading: of more than 600 criminal gangs examined, over 40 per cent deal in cannabis, half in cocaine and a similar number in heroin, and about 40 per cent in so-called 'synthetic' drugs such as ecstasy. All this means the big firms are raking in millions of pounds every week.

The Spanish government has regularly vowed that their police would seize assets if they could prove 'on the balance of probability' that gangsters were living off the proceeds of their crimes. The Spanish police even pushed for the power to grab dirty money from the bank accounts of major criminals involved with drugs, prostitution, money laundering, counterfeiting, smuggling or computer fraud. But the logistics of carrying out such high-tech measures have so far proved beyond the Costa del Sol police. One Spanish detective even admits, 'These criminals don't even hide their wealth, they flaunt it – especially the ladies of the family. Profit is the only thing that drives these people. Who knows when we'll arrest them in the end?'

Drugs money in Spain is laundered through reinvestment in pubs, restaurants, clubs and even 'car fronts' – open-air used-motor lots. Criminals also dip in and out of property deals, often working through specially set-up legitimate businesses. One well-known Costa del Sol property dealer who owed £600,000 to a gangster was shot dead after failing to come up with the cash.

Another little-known source of income for the big-name gangsters in southern Spain is the trade in counterfeit currency. A lot of villains have been swift to pick up on this. Barclays Bank recently intercepted more than £1 million worth of fake notes from Gibraltar, and it is reckoned that more than £200 million in forged euro cash is floating around at any one time.

The established criminals in Spain – Brits, Kurds, Russians, Eastern Europeans and Germans – all pose an enormous threat to safety on the streets and beaches of Spain because most of them are always armed. There is even a Chinese mafia which dabbles in drugs, people importation and protection rackets, mainly within its own Chinese community. Those who trade in people charge up to £10,000 per person, and this is now rivalling drugs as the most lucrative enterprise.

Spain is also fast becoming a key staging post for teams of African smugglers dealing in everything from people to drugs. Until recently, the Nigerians concentrated on complex frauds and benefit scams back in the UK, but in the Costa del Sol they already control 90 per cent of the heroin trade. British Customs and Excise and the National Criminal Intelligence Service (NCIS) have specialist squads monitoring and infiltrating African organised-crime gangs slipping into Spain.

I first became involved with the shady world of Spanish-based UK criminals some years ago when I was working on a book about road-rage killer and underworld kingpin Kenny Noye. At the time, I hardly knew the area that ran from Malaga west along the coast past Fuengirola and Marbella to Estepona and beyond. When I tracked down some real-life villains in Spain for my Noye book, they painted an extraordinary picture of a society within a society where criminals and police existed in their own worlds with their own rules. Flying into Malaga and then turning right at the motorway exit was the equivalent of driving into a vast, sun-soaked criminal hinterland. All roads in the Costa del Sol lead to this subculture, and it seems that virtually every murder has a link to the criminals who've made their fortunes here, mostly from drugs and vice. It is chilling to think that such a lawless society exists in the middle of our most popular tourist destination.

In this book, I've tried to take you, the reader, on an authentic, nail-biting roller-coaster ride through the full-on criminality of the area. The people I encountered combined the wit of *Alfie* with the cold-bloodedness and tangled domestic lives of *The Sopranos*. A lot of the villains I've come across in Spain are mildly amused by my book, despite the fact that it gives away a few tricks of the trade. They enjoy the kick of their world being featured in print, even though only their closest criminal associates would recognise their contributions. Some even believe my exposure of their world will bring them even more respect on 'the manor'.

On a number of occasions I broke the writer's golden rule: don't get too close to your subjects. I had a few threats from the family of one well-known criminal when they thought I was pushing my luck in the name of research. It ended with a sinister phone call: 'We might chop you up if you keep stickin' yer nose in our business.' But that was as far as it went, thank God. As another more friendly villain later told me, 'If they'd really been after you they would hardly have bothered to tell you first, would they?'

Not everyone I've written about in *Costa del Crime* is bad. They can be funny, vulnerable, even kind, and I've tried to portray every aspect of their lives rather than just the predictable hard-nosed stuff. Many of them are street-smart survivors doing what they know best. Others are victims of circumstance desperately trying to keep their heads above water simply by offering tourists what they want – with greater or lesser degrees of criminality. Down at the recently opened Mijas racecourse, thousands of Brits gather every weekend to recreate their own slice of 'back home' atmosphere and gamble away a fortune in the process. A few miles away, other boozy Brits favour a handful of beach bars where you can buy passports, UK driving licences and even Spanish registration plates to help avoid congestion charges back in London. These people spend their nights ducking and diving around the mean streets of southern Spain, and they see the world differently to the rest of us. You learn to survive by your instincts; you don't trust many people; you don't make light conversation because loose lips can sink ships; you spend each day thinking that your world may be shut down by a sneaky grass, a jealous lover or an angry punter; you devise ways and means of keeping ahead of the game.

It is a potent, explosive cocktail that all adds up to the Costa del Crime.

PROLOGUE

'Fat Stan' heaved his 22-stone frame up into the driver's seat of his son's Range Rover with great difficulty. He was more used to motoring around in his own vintage Roller, once owned by Frankie Vaughan. Just as he checked the time on his gold Rolex, a man holding a gun equipped with a silencer strolled alongside him in the car park of Malaga Airport. As Stan pleaded for his life, two shots rang out and his vast, blubbery body slumped against the dashboard. The gunman calmly walked to the nearest elevator and took it down to the arrivals car park without once looking back at the scene of carnage he'd just created. The police only found Fat Stan's obese body slumped in that Range Rover after complaints from motorists about a swarm of flies.

Welcome to the Costa del Sol. Rolling fields of olive

trees, converted *fincas*, golden beaches, glorious sunshine: it's supposed to be the perfect holiday resort area. Lively and bustling, it is filled with happy-go-lucky folk minding their own business, motivated by a love of the good life and everything that money can buy. But lurking among the whitewashed mansions and tower blocks are many of the biggest names in the criminal underworld. They are often multi-millionaires who describe themselves as 'businessmen' and 'property developers'; they deal strictly in cash.

Fat Stan, who once lived in a quiet village outside Dublin, was one of numerous villains who turned the Costa del Sol into the criminal badlands of Europe. Down the road from that airport lies Puerto Banus, perhaps the best example of where criminals have laid territorial stakes. For more than 25 years it has been home to many underworld kingpins.

With a population of 35,000 full-time residents, Puerto Banus has a disproportionately large number of mock-Spanish villas with long driveways, immaculate high brick walls, sophisticated closed-circuit television, electronically operated gates and at least two guard dogs on duty. One well-known villain called his Rottweilers Brinks and Mat after his most infamous criminal enterprise, and even had centrally heated kennels specially built for them.

In the mid-1980s, multi-million-pound drug deals took over from security-van robberies as the principal source of income for UK villains. Dozens of upwardly mobile drug barons, money launderers and handlers of stolen property turned the Spanish coastline into their number-one destination. Even when the UK government finally established a proper extradition treaty between the two countries, British villains who knew nothing could be proved against them stayed on.

'In many ways these people crave the respectability of living in a good neighbourhood,' says one retired British detective. 'A lot of them send their children to expensive boarding schools back in the UK. They have the same domestic aspirations as the rest of us, but they make their fortunes by breaking the law.'

At the other end of the criminal scale are the sex workers, lynchpins of the crime industry. They have turned the Costa del Sol into a place where anything goes, as many of the people interviewed for this book will testify. When I recently tried to talk to a brothel keeper called Bert and his wife through their electronically operated gates, I was greeted by two Dobermanns (I didn't catch their names) and a few terse words spoken through the crackling intercom. Bert's wife examined my face on her closed-circuit television screen, and then charmingly told me to 'fuck off'. Maybe I should have been more cautious, since another criminal had told me that Bert was not averse to throwing his weight around if the mood took him. A few months earlier he'd been down at one of his favourite pubs in Estepona port when a rival villain popped in for a pint. Bert was so infuriated he walked out to his Rolls Royce, pulled a shotgun out of the boot and stomped back into the tavern where he peppered the ceiling with pellets. Residents on Bert's street still talk about the day one of his Dobermanns strayed into a neighbour's garden and a string of angry complaints ensued. Bert accosted the Spanish neighbour, accused him of being a 'nark' – or informer – and threatened to 'bury' him. He didn't receive any more complaints about the dogs.

Living in the glorious Spanish sunshine doesn't guarantee a long and happy life if your business is crime. Only recently, a wealthy car dealer who specialised in selling cars with hard-to-trace Belgian number plates was found shot dead in his black BMW, slap bang in the middle of one of Marbella's most desirable residential areas.

Not all of the people featured in this book are on the wanted list, but many of them have thrived in the criminal atmosphere that has turned the Costa del Sol into a den of sex and crime. You are about to read stories that twist and turn through the mean streets, beaches and mountains that make up this extraordinary corner of Spain. It has been a fascinating journey, which I hope you are going to enjoy and relish as much as I have.

Just don't say you haven't been warned...

PART ONE
COSTA DEL CRIME

CHAPTER ONE
EVIL PREDATOR

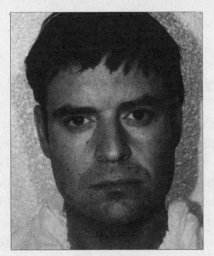

Richard Baker

EVIL PREDATOR

It has long been said that British girls pack their G-string bikinis and leave their morals at home when they venture down to the Costa del Sol. Potential dangers are routinely ignored, so it is perhaps small wonder that a nasty character called Richard Baker found life in Spain so congenial. Let this story be a sobering warning to the tens of thousands of single women who fly into the province of Malaga on holiday each year.

Richard Baker worked at numerous clubs and discos on the Costa del Sol, and is believed to have sexually assaulted more than a hundred victims. Baker started his career in Spain outside clubs, handing out leaflets promising cheap drinks. He later progressed to being a DJ. With his working hours stretching from early evening to 5 or 6am, Baker's job was demanding. The pay was poor, but there were a number of hidden 'perks'.

As one of Baker's pals on the Costa del Sol, a suntanned East Ender who calls himself Roberto, pointed out, 'We have a wicked time out here. It's like a supermarket for sex and drugs.' Roberto was later interviewed by Scotland Yard officers investigating allegations against Baker. 'All the girls who come here on holiday are always so pissed up they can barely remember anything the next morning,' he told them. 'That's the way it is out here.'

Baker liked using more than just alcohol to soften up his intended victims. He'd lure them into bars, buy them a drink and then, police believe, lace their cocktails with drugs. One of Baker's favourite hunting grounds was the *Paseo Maritimo*, which runs the length of the seafront at Fuengirola. During the daytime this area is alive with souvenir shops, ice-cream parlours and restaurants. But late at night this family atmosphere is replaced by hoards of drunken Brits wobbling along the promenade. The sound of the Mediterranean lapping on the sandy beaches is drowned out by the blazing disco systems of numerous clubs and bars with names like Old Town, Tramps, the Beetle Bar, the London Underground and the London Pub.

Baker liked to home in on women in such places. His speciality was chatting up girls in their late teens and early 20s who had come to Spain to forget about their mundane existences back in Britain. Jobs, boyfriends, family and responsibilities were pushed to the back of their minds as they went for it during frantic drinking binges on the seafront. By 11.30 most evenings, dozens of such young women were well on their way to oblivion.

As these girls consumed more and more alcohol, their dancing usually became more and more uninhibited. Baker later told friends that he believed such women were 'asking for it'. They were often plain girls who needed to be relaxed by alcohol before letting themselves go. Baker homed in on one girl after she clambered onto a tabletop, her tiny miniskirt riding high up her thighs. He watched as she and a friend gyrated on the table and even made gestures towards one another; legs apart and hips thrust forward, they performed an excruciating bump-and-grind routine, occasionally caressing them-selves and each other. As Baker's latest unsuspecting target smoothed her hands over her breasts and hitched up her tiny Lycra skirt, he cheered her on from the dance floor. He didn't care that the girl's performance was tawdry and embarrassing; he had already identified her as his next victim.

Eventually, driven by the need for another Bacardi and Coke, Baker's target stopped dancing and approached the bar. That's when he pounced. As she was paying for her drink, he appeared alongside her. She noticed him immediately thanks to his handsome, dark features, and grabbed him by the arm. 'Hey, don't I know you?' Baker smiled and nodded in agreement, happy in the knowledge that this young woman was too drunk to know any better.

He hadn't the faintest idea who she was. But as he took her hand and led her to a dark corner of the club, he believed that she was out for a good time and he was about to ensure she would be unable to escape his clutches. In the dingy, badly lit booth where they sat squeezed up against each other, she didn't notice him drop a pill into her Barcardi and Coke.

'Yeah, I know you,' yelled Baker above the din. Formalities over, the young girl lunged at Baker and the two were soon entwined in a passionate kiss. It wasn't until at least five minutes later that they came up for air. She took a huge gulp at her drink and their lips locked on each other once again.

Within 30 minutes, sexual predator Richard Baker was helping his latest victim out of the club and towards his nearby apartment, confident that she would soon be barely conscious, and unable to remember what he was about to do...

Baker was frequently out on the prowl for more victims. He specialised in clubs that were already packed. The strobe and ultraviolet lighting usually helped his *modus operandi* since many of his victims didn't even manage to get a proper look at his facial features before he went in for the kill. Many girls later recalled how the heady combination of alcohol, sometimes recreational drugs and bizarre lighting often left them feeling off kilter. They were unable to grasp the grim reality of what they were about to let themselves in for by allowing Baker to chat them up.

One of his favourite tricks was to approach a potential victim as they passed any of his favourite bars. He could even conjure up a plausible northern or Scottish accent just to make his target feel more at home. In any case, most of the girls were too drunk to pick up on any inconsistencies. Baker would often draw them in by explaining how he'd had some terrible bad luck. That would then make his young victims feel sympathy for him. He had his routine down pat. The girls usually believed him and that helped ease him on to stage two of his chilling rapist routine.

Baker later told one friend on the Costa del Sol that the easiest girls were the teenagers who wanted to be treated like grown-ups away from the watchful eye of their parents. One night, he engaged a pretty 16-year-old in conversation as he was handing out flyers on the pavement outside one of Fuengirola's most notorious nightclubs. As her two friends continued on into the club, Baker turned on all the charm and, combined with his obvious good looks, persuaded the young girl to meet him at another bar later that same night. He pointed out the location to the girl before she disappeared into the club to catch up with her friends.

A couple of drinks later, the girl emerged and headed for the bar where Baker was waiting. Within an hour he'd spiked her drink and had sex with her on a nearby beach. So much for having a laugh Costa del Sol style.

The unpleasant truth is that it is the Brits who have created the Costa culture of cheap drink, drugs and easy sex. Richard Baker was one of many who took full advantage of this. After more than three decades of British holidaymakers flooding into the area, even the locals hold their hands up in apathy. 'It's just the way it is out here,' says one veteran British resident. 'Of course Richard Baker was an appalling character, but in many ways we only have ourselves to blame for helping create such monsters.'

One of Baker's victims later recalled how she met the so-called DJ in a heaving Fuengirola club more than a year before his arrest for multiple rapes that took place back in the UK. Blonde and petite, she freely admits that until her encounter with Baker she enjoyed being the centre of attention. 'I was the type of girl who loved being grabbed by men the moment I walked into a crowded bar. It seemed like fun, and it made me feel much better about myself.'

The girl had spent the first few days of her holiday on the Costa del Sol with her best friend sitting round the pool at their hotel 'so we could get a decent tan before we went out pulling'. They both already had a poor opinion of Spanish men 'because they think English girls are easy'. No wonder it was so simple for Baker to chat her up when they first met.

On that night, the girl and her friend had been drinking whisky and lemonade, and vodka and Red Bull. They were draining their glasses and about to leave for another club when Baker approached. 'He looked gorgeous, and he was English so I trusted him immediately. He had the most amazing, penetrating eyes,' she later recalled. In the background, the disco was still going at full throttle: 'It's raining men,' went the song. 'It's raining men, hallelujah!'

An hour later, with the oceanfront streets of Fuengirola resembling a modern-day Sodom and Gomorrah, the girl found herself hand in hand with Richard Baker. 'He told me he knew a very nice little bar where we could sit and chat,' she later recalled. 'It sounded fine to me. I told my friend I'd see her back at the hotel.'

A hundred yards further down the road, the girl started to feel dizzy. 'I remember I looked across at him and he seemed to be smiling in my direction so I thought there couldn't be anything wrong.'

The next thing she remembered was waking up in Baker's bed the next morning. 'I was shocked, upset and burst into tears. He was sleeping next to me and didn't wake up. I grabbed my clothes and let myself out of the apartment. Luckily I managed to hail a passing taxi, which took me back to the hotel. I sobbed all day. I'd never slept with a man on a one-night stand, and I couldn't understand how I could get so out of control.'

It was only when the girl saw Baker's photo in the British press following his arrest in the UK that she realised she must have been one of his victims. 'It all made sense. I just wish I'd never gone to the Costa del Sol in the first place. The worst thing is that I'm sure he's not the only one doing that to girls on holiday.'

Many of the dodgy characters like Richard Baker on the Costa del Sol treat the place as if it is some kind of loophole in reality. 'These girls are on holiday. No one will know what they got up to back home, so what does it matter?' says Tommy, who has lived in Spain for 15 years and claims to have slept with thousands of girls. But why do so many women go so crazy on the Costa del Sol? Some say it's because they're bored of their mundane lives back home. For 50 weeks of the year they plod on, numb with tedium. Their reward is a fortnight of complete and utter madness. But is it really as simple as that?

Marie Stopes International recently revealed that demand for abortions in the UK rises sharply in August and September as young women return from holiday flings. Some say the hot climate on the Costa del Sol encourages the shedding of physical inhibitions. We wear fewer clothes, feel less constrained and more relaxed. And beaches are undoubtedly sexy places. But there's nothing particularly romantic about what many girls get up to on Spain's southern coast. Their behaviour suggests desperation: bored and disillusioned, these women seek solace in an uninhibited fantasy world. And it is a world where predators like Richard Baker thrive.

On 20 May 1999, Baker, 34, was found guilty of sexual assaults on 12 women in England; following a series of rape allegations from female holidaymakers, British police handed to Spanish police files on numerous assaults committed by Baker while on the Costa del Sol. They believe Baker assaulted more than a hundred victims.

CHAPTER TWO
ETA TERRORIST

Olaia Castresana

ETA TERRORIST

Attractive brunette Olaia Castresana loved little children and was training to be a kindergarten teacher, but her life ended up taking a very different course. In July 2001, at the age of 22, she blew herself up with her own bomb at a holiday apartment just one hour's drive from the Costa del Sol, sending masonry and chunks of her upper body flying on to bathers in the swimming pool below her.

Among the pimps, hookers, drug dealers and master criminals exists another, even more deadly threat on this popular slice of Spanish coastline: ETA terrorists. These people are not seedy ruffians living in squalid homes and sneaking around in the shadows. Terrorists such as Olaia openly pronounce themselves to be freedom fighters battling for a just cause. This young woman's middle-class parents knew full well that she lived, breathed and ultimately died for her dream of a united independent Basque state, made up of seven provinces currently belonging to Spain and France. It is worth briefly explaining the complex web of emotion and history that has turned ETA into one of the most lethal terrorist organisations in Europe. They want independence for the Basque region of northern Spain and have sworn to fight until the death to get their way. Their threat is omnipresent and their most prized target is the tourist industry on the Costa del Sol.

The story that detectives unravelled following Olaia's death provides a chilling warning to all visitors and residents on the Costa del Sol. It emerged that she and her school sweetheart Anartz Oiarzabal, had worked hard during the week and planted bombs at the weekends and during their holidays. They were part of a new generation of ETA activists, born in a democratic Spain that long ago gave a measure of self-government to its Basque region in the north, and prepared to kill and die for an impossible dream. Olaia and her boyfriend her bombing partner, were brought up in the elegant northern seaside city of San Sebastian, where violent separatism and chic opulence live side by side.

They learned their radical politics in their teens. Anartz, just one year older than his terrorist lover, and Olaia had been involved in separatist street fighting since they were 16 years of age. Both had respectable jobs – Anartz wore a suit and tie to his work at a funeral parlour. His parents were so wealthy that they owned the holiday apartment where Olaia was later to commit her final act of terrorism. Olaia's mother Ana explained shortly after her daughter's appalling death, 'She always said she wanted her ashes scattered over the seven provinces. Freedom fighting was her life and if the wealthy tourists in the south got in her way then so be it.' That calling had taken Olaia to the relatively quiet holiday town of Torrevieja, which lies to the east of the Malaga province. She had been briefed by her ETA bosses back in the north to contribute to the group's campaign against tourist targets. It was a campaign which, just days before her death, saw a potentially lethal car bomb planted at Malaga Airport. That particular bomb was located before it could explode, but the alert that evacuated the airport caused travel chaos for tens of thousands of British tourists.

Spanish police blamed the explosion that killed Olaia on the fact that ETA, which used to have teams of professional bombers, was now recruiting part-timers who supported themselves and led ordinary working lives. All this meant that Olaia had received just one weekend of training by ETA bomb-making experts. Olaia had not intended to become a martyr to her cause: she simply hadn't had enough training to prevent her making that final, fatal error.

While on the run after her death, Anartz contacted a separatist newspaper called *Gara* and placed a death notice to Olaia in large, bold print: I LOVE YOU.

A year earlier, Olaia's ETA colleagues had assassinated a politician in Malaga. Since then, other bombings along the popular resorts of Torremolinos and Fuengirola have caused numerous injuries to innocent bystanders. The message ETA continues to issue to British visitors and residents on the Costa del Sol is blunt: travel to Spain at your own risk.

Police in Marbella reckon that ETA will target the Costa del Sol even more in coming years because any disruption they can cause will damage the area's all-important and lucrative tourist trade. 'It's a vicious circle,' says one highly ranked detective. 'Tourists are soft targets, but by scaring them away from here ETA can cause financial damage where it really hurts. That way they hope to get action from the government.'

ETA's new weekend and holiday killers are expected to integrate themselves into the Costa del Sol every summer. Police believe that the threat increases as each year passes. 'ETA is recruiting more and more of these part-timers and forming small cells with ordinary people who do not stand out in a crowd,' said one detective. Malaga police claim that anti-terrorist-squad officers monitor a lot of these cells, but admit they cannot keep track of them all the time. 'The danger comes when we lose them on our radar. That's when they are most likely to plant bombs and it's impossible to know who they all are and watch them all the time.'

ETA makes no secret of its obsession with attacking Spanish resort areas each summer. Back in March 2001, the group warned as much in a communiqué after a bomb killed a policeman in the Costa Brava beach town of Rosas. Olaia and her lover Anartz are suspected of having planted that bomb as well.

ETA has even told visitors to Spain to stay away from 'Spanish tourist economy objectives'. Their message is aimed specifically at European tourists who spend their holidays in these regions. These threats were further confirmed when an ETA commando was captured in the northern port of Santander in June 2001. A ferry to Plymouth had been on his list of targets.

The Malaga Airport bomb, which caused so much travel disruption in the summer of 2001, was by no means the first time ETA has targeted the Costa del Sol. Thirty-five British and Irish tourists were all seriously injured by flying glass when another device exploded at a smaller airport in a province to the east of Malaga in 1996.

One of the biggest fears is that the constant ETA threat will start to shrink tourism on the Costa del Sol. 'If they keep coming back year after year many people are going to stop coming here, it's as simple as that,' Rafael Prados, president of the Malaga Hoteliers Association, said after the 2001 Malaga Airport bomb alert, which delayed 193 flights. The British Foreign Office became involved during 2003 by telling tourists to be wary of strange packages, but they also pointed out you were much more likely to die on a Spanish road than in an ETA bomb blast.

Those close to ETA claim that the separatists have always tried to be careful to target buildings and beaches rather than people. But as the death of Olaia Castresana showed, bombs do not always behave as they are meant to. Up in the Basque stronghold of San Sebastian, separatists still talk in glowing terms about the 22-year-old martyr to the cause and insist that her death has inspired future generations of ETA bombers. But even if Olaia had not died at such a young age, she would probably never have lived to see the seven provinces become a single, independent country because realistically only two of them – the Spanish provinces of Guipuzcoa and Vizcaya – stand a chance of ever changing hands, and they would only get a limited amount of self-governement. 'It's a battle without a realistic aim,' says one terrorism expert. 'But ETA have proved the deadliest terrorists in European history and it's almost as if they have forgotten the reasons why they were formed in the first place.'

As one Malaga policeman pointed out recently, 'Down here in the south of Spain we have no interest in terrorism; we just want a quiet, peaceful life. But there is a very real fear that ETA will one day slaughter a lot of tourists and the tide will turn for the Costa del Sol.'

CHAPTER THREE
BAD GIRLS

Anne-Marie Monteith

BAD GIRLS

The story of the British mother of five who spent more than a year in a Spanish prison on a murder charge, which has since been dropped, represents the ultimate Costa del Sol nightmare. Anne-Marie Monteith, 48 and hailing from Monkseaton in Whitley Bay, was first arrested in March 2002. She claims she was chained to her bed for hours on end after refusing the sexual advances of two female prison officers at the jail in the town of Alhaurin de la Torre, just 20 miles north of Malaga. 'What I've just been through makes *Bad Girls* look like a holiday camp,' she explained. 'I was humiliated and treated no better than an animal. It was a disgusting, horrible nightmare that has damaged me for life.

'Being chained to the bed was the worst thing of all. These two particular members of staff accused me of insolence when I refused to sleep with one of them. Then they came into my cell late one night and handcuffed me to the bed. They did that for the following ten days each night. When I asked why, they said it was for my own protection.'

Inside the prison where Anne-Marie was held were just a hundred females inmates and well over a thousand men. 'They were in the other half of the prison and we had little direct contact with the men, apart from drama classes. But just the fact they were so close made things a bit tricky.'

Anne-Marie says that drama classes she attended inside the prison 'were awful, because the men were allowed to sit next to us and some of them would try and molest us under the tables. Some women inmates were happy to allow the men to fondle them, but I was disgusted. I just don't understand why they were allowed to do it. The staff spent the whole time smirking at us.'

Anne-Marie is convinced she was discriminated against because she was English. 'They thought I was an easy lay because that's what they think of English women. It was terrifying. There were many hardened criminals in there for robbery and drugs, and a lot of sick perverts. The prison was only fifteen years old but it was in desperate need of a revamp. It was disgusting. I wouldn't have put an animal in there. The toilets were broken, cracked and unfit for human use, and excrement was spread across the floor. The walls of the cell were peeling and cracked and the smell was disgusting throughout the prison.'

She claims she only took a shower twice throughout her year in the prison because 'you had to watch your clothes in case any of the inmates stole them. Also, I felt that someone might try and force me to have sex. And the water was a disgusting brown colour.'

Back in the main part of the prison things were no better. 'Sometimes squads of male prison officers would come into our unit to stop a fight, and they were always very violent. Some of the women inmates were beaten for just waving at the male inmates in the next-door jail.'

Anne-Marie says she was stunned by the open nature of the sexual relations between women inmates and sometimes even the staff. 'Many of the women inmates had sex with each other in their cells and they were constantly kissing and caressing each other in the refectory and TV areas. It was very offensive because of the way they defiantly did it in front of you, but none of the staff ever stopped them. In fact, three or four women staff members were having open relationships with female inmates. There was also a woman who was close to death with AIDS who walked around trying to pick fights with us. It was awful.'

There were regular scuffles between female inmates. 'They'd suddenly go for each other's throats. There were fist fights, catfights everything, you name it. They'd tear each other's hair out and many of the inmates urged them on, getting some sick and twisted kick out of it all.'

But the most humiliating moment came when Anne-Marie was allowed a conjugal visit from her husband

Richard. 'I was allowed to see him through a glass panel twice a month for an hour, but then they permitted us a conjugal visit. We went in the room. It was bare with tiles on the walls, a little cubicle to wash in, a toilet and nothing else. No curtains on the window. The chipboard bed creaked so badly that in the end we had to stop. I could hear the prison staff sniggering just outside the door. It was so inhibiting. I told my husband I could never do it again because it was so humiliating.'

Anne-Marie also believes prison staff deliberately called her by her surname even though most other inmates were referred to by their Christian name. 'It was their way of further humiliating me because I was the only English woman in the prison.'

Random strip-searches convinced Anne-Marie she was being completely and utterly victimised. 'They would stop me in the middle of the recreation area and force me to drop my pants in front of everyone. It was disgusting. They claimed they were looking for drugs but I think they just did it for sick, twisted and perverted reasons. It was horrible.'

Anne-Marie insists she never once took any drugs throughout her stay in the prison. 'Drugs got in so easily. Women had them in their knickers. Others exchanged them through kisses and hand squeezing. There were even certain pushers inside the prison trying to force you to buy the drugs from them. Many women inmates would go down to the showers, crush the drugs into cigarettes and then get high. They even used tablets from the medical wing. Anything to get high.'

She claims she was locked in solitary confinement inside her cell for calling an officer 'stupid'. 'I wasn't allowed out. I used the toilet and wash-basin and my meals were brought to the cell, all because I called one of the women officers who was harassing me "stupid".'

Anne-Marie was finally released from prison in March 2003 after police found clear evidence that she had not been involved in the murder of a wealthy British housewife called Diana Dyson on the Costa del Sol in December 2001. Anne-Marie's husband Richard remains in a Spanish jail awaiting trial for the murder, but his case is not expected to be heard for at least another year. 'I cannot believe that it took so long to release me. Now I have to battle to try and get Richard released because he is as innocent as I am.'

Anne-Marie claims that the real killer of elderly Mrs Dyson is another Brit who has now returned to the north-east of England. 'But the Spanish police are doing nothing to try and extradite this man. I am so worried about my husband. He is completely innocent.'

CHAPTER FOUR

DIAMOND GEEZER

Max Diamond

DIAMOND GEEZER

The Costa del Sol throws up some very unlikely characters with some peculiar names, but the man who really takes the biscuit in this department is Max Diamond. Yes, that really is his name. Max is a man for all seasons, and he's got a finger in every pie, working very hard making an honest living. This 44-year-old from the Midlands is one of the most familiar faces in Benalmadena, a popular resort sandwiched between Fuengirola and Torremolinos. From his offices on the ground floor of a high-rise apartment building, he is unashamedly trying to cash in on the Brits who have swamped the area over the past 20 years.

His latest business enterprise is something called freeonlineshops.com, a wonderfully simple idea that he hopes will help make him millions – and it's legit. It comes in the wake of another money-spinner: an online tobacco-supply service that takes advantage of Spain's ludicrously cheap cigarettes, which are shipped out to the UK through orders on the internet.

With a string of young girlfriends and a couple of children by other women, Max has to earn a decent wedge to meet all his monthly commitments; his efforts to make a bob or two sum up what is needed to make a straight success of your life out on the dodgy old Costa del Crime. 'Something happens to you when you get out here. You lose all sense of proportion compared to what you were used to back home,' he explains, and he's not just talking about his business acumen. 'It must be the sun, the booze and the women, but so many blokes come a cropper and get hooked on all three.'

Max doesn't hide the fact he's a liberal-thinking swinger, just as happy wandering through the corridors of the local wife-swap club as he is propping up his local bar with a pint of lager in a straight glass. 'Anything goes out here. It's bloody brilliant. I've never had sex with so many women in such a short space of time.' At the time of writing, after just five years on the Costa del Sol, Max puts his conquests at the thousand-plus mark. He reckons he's tried it all: threesomes, foursomes, orgies. You name it, Max seems to have done it. But there's something refreshingly honest about him. He is open about what he does and insists he's not ashamed of anything. 'Why should I hide the fact I like sex with lots of different women all the time? Is it such a big deal? I don't think so. It's only all the frigid, rigid people back in Middle England who want to ruin all the fun by making disapproving remarks. They're just frustrated by their own lack of opportunity. Out here, no one cares what your sexual persuasion is. People have the spirit to do exactly what they want, and they do just that.'

Max doesn't even hide the fact that at least two of his girlfriends have worked in Costa del Sol brothels in the recent past. 'Sure, I met them in brothels. Why should I hide that? They are normal human beings like the rest of us. Just because they're paid to have sex with men doesn't mean they're not worthy of a proper relationship.'

Underneath the brash exterior lies a sensitive soul who is always willing to give someone the benefit of the doubt. 'I don't judge people. Who am I to say whether someone is good or bad? I start every relationship with an open mind and I don't care about anyone's past.'

Max openly admits to being a regular customer at many of the coast's most notorious brothels – or clubs, as he calls them. 'There's nothing I like better than going down to a few clubs on a Saturday night and having a good time. There are some amazing girls in those places. Many of them are a lot brighter than some of the women you find in the bars round here.'

And if he's seeing someone at the time, it makes no difference – Max simply doesn't see it as cheating. 'I don't understand what that word really means. I always tell my girlfriends when I go to the clubs because I don't think it's fair to lie like most men. Surely it's better to be honest about it?'

The swinging scene in Benalmadena and surrounding areas can be perfectly summed up by Max's old mate

Pete, who openly admits to an orgy or t
'Me and the wife have found it has given o
real boost. It's a very active scene out here. Even
couples are now turning up at clubs and there's also
or two Spanish-only swingers' clubs along the coast
which have opened up recently. Funny thing is that,
until all the Brits and Germans turned up a few years
back, they didn't even know what swinging meant.'

Max and his staff of internet pioneers often enjoy a
staff outing to one local swingers' club called Eden
Rock, which operates out of a basement just a stone's
throw from the sandy beaches that are filled every
summer with tens of thousands of holidaymakers. Max
freely admits to being a regular at the club, which is just
a short walk from the centre of Benalmadena. 'I love it
down there. Sometimes you can walk in and the place is
really heaving. There are couples having sex up against
the bar, men watching couples having sex in side rooms,
and women seducing each other in the corridors. It's
fantastic. Out of this world. It's a brilliant way to break
down barriers because once you get in the place you
have to either join in or leave. There are no half
measures. You'd be amazed at how many women
completely lose their inhibitions once they're inside
Eden Rock. Some of the straightest-looking people turn
into the most sex-hungry vixens once they get into the
swing of things. It's as if there's a switch goes on in their
head once they walk through the door, and they become
desperate for sex.'

...s in the middle of what is
...pressing area. The streets
...e filled with tatty tower
...low-rent housing to British
...children who have relocated
...they are still claiming the
...he local resident who has lived
...elieves that fewer than half of
those ... o school. 'It's a bloody disgrace.
Sometimes it feels ... e most of Britain's white-trash
population have upped sticks and decided to opt for a
jobless life out here in the sun. Some days I walk out of
my house to be greeted by gangs of British kids loitering
on the street corners. And they're often still there late
into the night.'

Even easygoing Max admits that Benalmadena doesn't
exactly give out a glamorous impression: 'All the
lowlifes from back home seem to have been dumped on
Benalmadena's doorstep. Everywhere you look are these
single-mother types with their tearaway kids. They
come over here because it seems cheaper to live, but it's
getting dearer by the day. I just wish a lot of them would
go home and leave us all alone.'

Running a business like Max's on the Costa del Sol is
not easy. 'There are so many dodgy characters out here
that you've really got to watch your back. I get fellows
coming into my office offering me all sorts of things –
pirate videos, stolen furniture from the Far East, even
lighters that don't have a flame. Luckily, I've developed
a sixth sense from dealing with that sort of person and I

can spot them a mile away. But you constantly have to watch your back because some of these people are police informants, and if you buy anything from them the law turns up at your doorstep the next day.'

Max rarely has time to unwind at his rented three-bedroom house up in the hills overlooking Benalmadena. 'I start work early and finish late. Most people here have a siesta between two and five in the afternoon, but because I'm dealing with internet customers over in the UK there's no time for even a brief lunch break. By the time I finish up in the evening it's at least nine and I often go straight out for a bite to eat followed by a few drinks and maybe a visit to a local club to meet a girl, depending on my mood.'

But Max prides himself on keeping away from some of the heavier British criminal elements who are constantly trying to poke their noses into many of Benalmadena's business enterprises. 'It's a mess down here. There are a lot of British scumbags who come down and try to reinvent themselves as big-time villains. We've got one character out here who thinks he's Al Capone. He's knocking off rival villains at a rate of three or four a month and he seems to be completely out of his mind on charley the whole time. The guy's a tinderbox. We're just hoping the law catches up with him before he does some real damage to innocent people.'

Max's own *modus operandi* is 'to keep a low profile, earn an honest crust and stay out of the way of all the troublemakers. I've tried my hand at most things, and the biggest problem out here is to get people to take you seriously. The Costa del Sol is my life and I genuinely believe that there are many amazing opportunities here, but you've got to fight your way through all the bullshit first to find the light at the end of the tunnel.'

CHAPTER FIVE

DARREN THE
DRUG DEALER

'Darren'

DARREN THE DRUG DEALER

The sinister, shadowy figures who run the Costa del Sol's illicit drugs trade tend to remain well out of the limelight. But the so-called 'soldiers' who deliver their goods to the population have no choice but to expose themselves to all and sundry.

Take Darren, originally from Southend in Essex. He's been on the coastline flogging charley – that's cocaine to you and me – since fleeing the UK after, he claims, three of his mates were 'taken off the scene' by drug lords who control the supplies of ecstasy and cocaine throughout Essex.

Darren works all the popular hotspots between Torremolinos and Fuengirola, and his job has brought him into contact with a weird and not-so-wonderful collection of reprobates. His current customers include one of Britain's most famous TV entertainers, a homicidal gangster who takes coke virtually 24 hours a day and some of the most chilling villains you're ever likely to encounter. This is a world where you can walk into a certain beach bar and get offered a false passport within minutes, and Darren's patch includes some gruesome bars and clubs frequented almost exclusively by the trashiest Brits on the Costa del Sol.

He knows he's lucky to have survived thus far. 'It's a dodgy old game, there's no denying it, but it's what I pay the bills with.' Darren swears blind he never takes the produce himself. 'It's much better that way, because when the punters start moaning about the poor quality, I've got the perfect reply: "Sorry, mate. Never take the stuff myself." It soon stops them complaining.'

When Darren packed his bags and fled Essex back in 1996, he admits he didn't have a clue where he was heading. 'To tell you the truth, I thought about Thailand at first because it's so far away. Then I remembered a few fellas I knew down on the Costa del Sol, so I headed down here. It's all right, really. Sometimes I miss home, but there's so many familiar faces down here it's not that different from Essex, is it?'

At first, insists Darren, he ran a little 'puff' (cannabis) for a well-known British gangster who was on the run at the time but was trying to earn a crust by financing cannabis deals out of Morocco. 'It was a piece of cake back then,' explains Darren. 'The Spanish Old Bill never came near us because they were more concerned with the heavy stuff like coke and E, so we was left to our own devices.'

But then Darren's boss was tracked down by British police and deported back to the UK. 'That was a real blow,' says Darren. 'No one wanted to touch anyone connected to this bloke because the law were crawling all over him and his fellas. I not only found myself out of a job, but no one would touch me with a bargepole.'

Darren eventually got himself a straight job working in a bar in Torremolinos, but the money was poor and soon those familiar old temptations started nagging at him. 'I started flogging charley to a few select customers without the bar owner knowing. It was always going to end in tears, but the money was fucking good.' Eventually he was shopped by the bar owner to the police and slung in jail. 'It was a fucking nightmare. Spanish prisons are not nearly as nice as the ones in the UK. Creepy crawlies, filthy bogs. It was a hellhole.'

Then Darren had a stroke of luck. 'The bar owner keeled over and died from a heart attack. The police dropped the case against me because they couldn't trace any of my so-called customers. I was a free man, but back to square one. And everyone knew what I'd been banged up for so it was impossible to get another straight job.'

So he decided to set himself up as a full-time cocaine dealer. It was 1999 and he soon found that demand for charley had gone up even in the short time since he'd been in jail. 'It was an epidemic – and it still is. Everyone wants charley these days. It's not about rich people any more. Down here, everyone from the waiters in the restaurants to royalty want coke.' Within a year, he was selling more than a hundred grams of cocaine every week, representing a profit of at least £5,000. And he now admits, 'In truth, I cut my cocaine with other stuff like milk powder and that stretched it out so I could almost double my profits. I'd never been richer in my life.'

These days, Darren subcontracts out to runners – small-time dealers who deliver by car within a ten-mile radius of Fuengirola and nearby coastal resorts. 'I don't need to bother with all that small-time stuff, so I sell on the produce to the runners and keep a load back for my really big customers.'

And by 'big customers', Darren is referring to royalty, multi-millionaire local businessmen and major-league gangsters. 'These people want twenty to fifty grams a time. That's the sort of decent money I'm interested in.' He undoubtedly gets a kick from being welcomed into the homes of the rich and famous to see how the other half lives. 'It's funny really, because these people have to be nice to me otherwise they'd be fucked. I love it when they offer me a drink, and sometimes I even meet their families. Makes me feel important. I like that. I like that very much.'

But Darren is realistic enough to know that the longer he works as a drug dealer, the more likely it is he'll get caught out one day. 'No one gets nicked in this game because of bad luck. It's always because some bastard's grassed them up. That's the only way the Old Bill stand a chance. They nick the weak link and put him – or her – under the thumbscrews until they crack. That's when I'll get problems.'

In the summer of 2003, Darren had a close shave for a different reason when the teenage son of one major villain tried to score cocaine from him. 'That was right dodgy, because I knew that if his old man knew I was supplying his kid, I'd be for the chop, so to speak. And this kid was a right mean 'un, just like his dad, and put me under a load of pressure to supply him. In the end I fobbed him off with one of my runners and just about managed to distance myself from the whole thing, but that crim would have topped me if he'd known I was involved. There are certain lines you must not cross in this game.'

Now Darren lives in a swish penthouse flat, runs six different mobile phones and drives a top-of-the-range British-registered BMW 7 Series. 'It's better to keep British plates – then you never get parking tickets,' he reckons. Darren says he uses so many different phones because 'the law can't be bothered to monitor them all'.

Like so many characters on the Costa del Sol, Darren insists he's saving all his hard-earned loot and will one day 'split for good'. 'It's all right here. But to be honest about it, I need to get away before the law nabs me. I've had a couple of close shaves and I know they're keeping an eye on me. I've got to be careful.'

Underneath his brash exterior, Darren has the same aims as all the rest of us, but he has learned that the only thing money cannot buy is true love. He says he's been through dozens of girlfriends. 'They've all been English, but the trouble is most of them were more interested in me buying them a pair of the latest Gucci boots than settling down. I want a wife and kids. I don't want to be in this game for the rest of my life. I'd like to buy a small hotel up in the mountains behind Malaga, live a nice, simple life and forget about all this shit. But I'm caught in a trap. Lots of money, good lifestyle. It's going to be difficult to give up.'

For a short while last year, Darren thought he might have found the love of his life when he began dating a minor British soap actress he met when she was on holiday near Fuengirola. 'She was a good kid. I told her I was an estate agent and she believed it for a while. Then one of her mates heard on the grapevine that I was flogging gear. Next thing I know, she's dropped me like a stone. Pity. I really liked her.'

Some of Darren's friends have urged him to quit the drugs trade before it's too late. He takes a philosophical view. 'I'll know when it's actually time to quit. I've thought about it enough. It's just a matter of timing. When you start thinking about quitting every moment of the day, that's when you've got to get out because you're vulnerable and liable to get nicked.'

He paused for a moment to take a long sip of his vodka and Coke. 'But for the moment, I think luck's on my side. I'm going to keep saving all this loot for a rainy day. I'll be all right. I think.'

CHAPTER SIX
HOLIDAY HORROR

The area where the O'Malleys
were kidnapped

HOLIDAY HORROR

Tens of thousands of Brits flood to the Spanish coast every year looking for their dream place in the sunshine. They look on it as the perfect destination: safe, warm, friendly and not too far from home. Typical of these tourists were Anthony and Linda O'Malley, a car dealer and shop manager, respectively, who had long dreamed of owning a place in the sun. The O'Malley case deserves to be recounted here as a warning to those looking for sunshine homes anywhere in Spain.

'They'd been talking about and planning a move for ages,' Anthony's brother Bernard explained. 'They were always looking in estate agents' windows when they went out to Spain. They had their hearts set on a nice villa, away from the hustle and bustle of the tourist resorts. They wanted to get in touch with the real Spain in a rural village where they could settle down and enjoy a long retirement.'

When the O'Malleys set out for yet another visit to Spain in September 2002, their sole intention was to find that dream house. Halfway through the trip Linda, 55, phoned her daughter Jenny to remind her to post a birthday card to her brother-in-law. 'She sounded in good spirits and said that they were very hopeful they'd find the perfect villa,' Bernard O'Malley later recalled.

Anthony and Linda eventually spotted an isolated property overlooked by a vast mountain range, which seemed the perfect place to retire one day; perhaps they could set up a business and live happily ever after. The *casa* was located in the picturesque village of Alcoy, 12 miles inland from Benidorm. The O'Malleys had seen the property through an advertisement in an English-language newspaper, the *Costa Blanca News*, which referred to the villa being in a 'peaceful and very discreet area'. Tony and Linda immediately and enthusiastically responded to the advert. After the O'Malleys' first visit to the house, they were hooked. 'They must have been so excited. Suddenly their dream was about to come true,' Linda's daughter Jenny later explained.

But that dream home turned into the ultimate nightmare within a week of Linda's last phone call home. The couple disappeared into thin air, and then thousands of pounds were withdrawn from their joint bank account, followed by an extravagant spending spree on their credit cards. Back in Britain, relatives waited in vain for them to return to Manchester Airport; their hire car was never returned at Malaga.

For six months, the mystery of what happened to the O'Malleys remained unsolved. Had one partner murdered the other and then run away? Or had they just done a 'Shirley Valentine' and disappeared into the Spanish wilderness?

'The rumours were awful and very hurtful to the family, because they were both good people. We knew something dreadful must have happened,' said Jenny.

The O'Malleys' cash cards were used to buy a digital camera, a tape recorder, an infrared alarm, and clothes. The cards were only cancelled on 19 September, almost a week after they were supposed to have returned to the UK from Spain.

After that, the trail went completely cold. Spanish police even eventually scaled down the search for the missing couple amid speculation that they might have chosen to disappear. Bernard refused to believe the gossip and travelled to Spain three times to try and find the couple and bring them home. 'I always believed that while there was no news there remained that small glimmer of hope,' Bernard later recalled.

In March 2003, Spanish police working with officers in Wales struck lucky after discovering the couple's rented Fiat Stilo at El Saler, six miles south of Valencia on the country's eastern coastline. The number plate had been changed, but they tailed the driver back to a nearby apartment and kept him under surveillance for weeks before arresting him and his accomplice. Police then uncovered a string of documents linking the pair to the O'Malleys' disappearance, including passports, bank cards and two replica guns. The man and his brother-in-law had rented the house the O'Malleys wanted to buy with their wives and three children.

Then one of the suspects made a startling confession: he and his accomplice had murdered the O'Malleys and buried their bodies in the cellar of the villa they had advertised for sale the previous summer. Two men, named only as Jorge RS, 53, and José Antonio UG, 38, both from Venezuela in South America, were arrested and charged with the O'Malleys' murder. The suspects' wives were initially arrested with them, but later released to look after their three children at a secret location.

Gradually, the story began to be pieced together. The O'Malleys had been kidnapped a few days before their scheduled return to Britain on 13 September 2002. Anthony was forced to withdraw money by his captors while his wife was kept locked in the cellar of the house. The £18,000 taken from their Spanish bank account had just been deposited by the couple, who planned to put it down on their dream house. Another £30,000 was stripped from the O'Malleys' UK accounts before their bank put a block on all transactions. It was at this point, according to detectives, that the couple were brutally murdered in the 18 x 8-feet cellar of the house they had thought was going to become their dream holiday home. Their bodies were then buried in the earth that formed the floor of the cellar before a thick layer of concrete was poured over them and the floor painted red.

Detectives accompanied one suspect to the villa and the bodies were found after officers used pneumatic drills and spades to dig through the concrete to the hole where the bodies of the O'Malleys lay. As local police chief José Abellan explained, 'If we hadn't been led to the spot, we would never have found them.'

Police believe the two suspects, who had both lived in Spain since 1974, showed the O'Malleys around the property with the original intention of simply robbing them. A local police spokesman explained, 'After that, for reasons we are still investigating, they moved on to kidnap and then murder. We believe they may also have carried out numerous similar crimes.'

As Juan Cortino, government commissioner for the region, later explained, 'It was the kind of place the O'Malleys had been looking for. We believe they visited it two or three times, and on their last visit they were kidnapped.' At a press conference shortly after the arrest of the Venezuelans, police played a disturbing video recording of one of the suspects arriving at the villa in handcuffs and then leading detectives to the place where the O'Malleys were buried. Police then revealed that Anthony had been asphyxiated with a plastic bag; his wife had been strangled to death.

It even emerged that police had located CCTV footage, which showed Anthony being frogmarched to a cash machine by one of the Venezuelans. Local town hall official Juan Cortino said the whole community was shocked by the murders. 'Not only do they kill them, but before they kill them they keep them hostage with extortion in mind.'

Evidence that the couple had been tortured emerged when police found a combined truncheon and electric cattle prod in the flat in Valencia.

Bernard knew it was going to be bad news when the local police in North Wales came knocking at his door. 'We had been hoping against hope that they might be alive. It's heartbreaking to think they were planning a new life and it ended up costing them their lives. It was sheer hell waiting to hear what had happened to them. And it is horrible to think how they were killed.'

In a statement, Detective Sergeant Steve Lloyd of North Wales Police said, 'We are pleased the families have got some sort of closure, although it's obviously not the outcome we would have hoped for. We have no evidence to suggest the suspects have indeed robbed or murdered other Britons. But that is something the Spanish police will be looking into.'

The investigation has now been passed to three judges and is likely to take several months to complete. The trial of the two men is not expected to be heard until the end of 2004. As Anthony O'Malley's brother Bernard succinctly put it, 'Anthony and Linda were a real love match. The pair of them had their hearts set on a nice villa, away from the hustle and bustle of the tourist resorts. But that dream – and their lives – have been snatched away from them for a few thousand pounds.'

CHAPTER SEVEN

A SHADY SPANISH UNDERTAKING

Juan Lanzat Cubus

A SHADY SPANISH UNDERTAKING

While our boys were liberating Iraq in the early months of 2003, a group of British war heroes who helped fight off the worldwide threat to peace during WWII were being cruelly duped by a cold-hearted Costa del Sol undertaker in the resort of Benalmadena, who ran off with more than £40,000 of their money. The ex-servicemen's association and their families had put the cash into a special fund so that, in the event of their deaths, funeral expenses would be automatically paid rather than creating financial problems for relatives back in the UK. Now many of them face being given the serviceman's ultimate insult – a pauper's funeral – because the fund to pay for their burial or cremation was stolen by smooth-talking Latino undertaker Juan Lanzat Cubus.

'These people are war heroes. It's scandalous,' said local ex-servicemen's association secretary Frank Voyce, who put £1,300 of his own money into the scheme. He believes Spanish conman Cubus is an evil man. Mr Voyce, 78, originally from Bedford, encouraged 29 members each to pay between £1,300 and £1,500 into a special fund that was to cover the cost of a coffin, hearse, death certificate, cemetery fees, a funeral service, two days of cold storage and flowers. Undertaker Cubus was even contractually obliged to contact relatives back in the UK. 'The idea was to take the pressure off our relatives back in the UK so that when we died they wouldn't be landed with the costs,' explained Frank, who served with the Royal Fusiliers when they helped liberate Italy in 1945.

'It seemed a splendid scheme and Señor Cubus even came to two of our dinner dances to meet us. He was charming and we never once doubted his sincerity. He even danced with two elderly ladies who were most taken by him. I just cannot believe that someone could be so cruel.'

The funeral of Winifred Carter-Humphries, 91 and the widow of a Navy petty officer, had to be paid for by her impoverished sister because Cubus had shut down his business and disappeared without paying back the servicemen and women who'd contributed to the special funeral fund. Winny's sister Kate Bale, 86, whose own husband, Reginald, served in the army during WWII, said, 'It's been a really awful time. Not only has my sister died, but I've had to pay out almost £2,000 for Winny's funeral, which was virtually all my savings. I live on a £310-a-month pension. It's going to be very difficult to survive from now on. That man is a cruel, heartless fellow for taking all our money.'

Frank only stumbled upon the con when he tried to contact Cubus after Winny Carter-Humphries was struck down by a serious stroke in 2003 and it quickly became clear that it was unlikely she would ever recover so the Legion's special fund would have to be used after her death. Frank explained, 'Cubus's office phone had been cut off so I went to Malaga and was stunned to discover that his office and showroom had been shut down. When I tried to find him, his family said he'd disappeared. Then I found his brother, who told us that he wasn't to be trusted. Alarm bells immediately started ringing.'

At the shop and office in Malaga city centre's Calle de Comedias where Cubus ran his company Funeria Malaguena, the new tenants said that fraudster Cubus had closed down his operation in December 2002 without even providing a forwarding address. One of the tenants said, 'Juan owes a lot of people money and we don't even know where he has gone.'

One man, José Cascido, who used to work for Cubus, said, 'I am not surprised to hear that Cubus has deceived these people. He is a heartless man who owes money to many people. I hate him. He never paid me my last few months of salary and I will do anything to help the British Legion. I am suing Cubus myself in the courts later this year.'

Nobody knew where Cubus had gone, or how to find him. So I decided to track him down myself...

I located the evil swindler at his luxurious £400,000 detached home in one of Malaga's smartest suburbs. A brand-new £18,000 Volkswagen was parked in the driveway. I confronted him. Cubus shrugged his shoulders and said, 'I have nothing to hide. I will meet Señor Voyce and talk to him. There has been a misunderstanding.' Over the following few months I checked with Frank Voyce to see if he had ever heard from Cubus. Not even a phone call was received.

Later, when I again asked Cubus if he'd pay British Legion associated members back all their cash, the dishonest Spaniard said, 'I still have to talk to Señor Voyce. I am sure we can sort this out. I have opened another funeral company in Malaga and we will honour our obligations to the ex-servicemen.' And so, in the middle of our confrontation, I telephoned Frank. Cubus refused to take the phone and talk to him directly, but once again promised to call him later that same day.

But Frank was not afforded the courtesy of the promised phone call. 'I never heard a word from him. We all know what his game is, and he is nothing more than a cheap conman who ought to be ashamed of himself.'

When I visited the location where Cubus claimed he'd opened a new office, there was no sign of a funeral company in the entire building. One office worker in the small block said, 'I've never heard of this man, and there has never been a funeral company here.'

Even Cubus's parents, Juan, 68, and Encarna, 66, who live in the isolated village of Casabermeja, 20 miles north of Malaga, say they have washed their hands of their son. 'Juan appears here sometimes but he never tells us what he is doing and we don't even have a telephone number for him,' explained the father.

In the village, many locals know Juan Cubus by his reputation. They remember his involvement in another undertaker's scam, which brought him to the attention of local police back in 2000. It seems the company he ran was pretending to cremate bodies but was, in fact, sending them to another province in Spain where they were destroyed at a much lower cost, leaving him with more profit. He would then present grieving relatives with a pot of ash.

One old friend and neighbour of the family in Casabermeja said, 'Juan is the black sheep of the family. We all knew about his scam with the bodies a couple of years ago, but to take money from these old British servicemen is even more disgusting. We hope he never shows his face around here again.'

British Legion lawyer Eleanor Smith described Cubus as a 'classic conman'. 'I understand that Cubus was involved with the company that pretended to cremate the bodies and then sent them to Seville where they were destroyed at a much cheaper cost to the company, giving them more profit. They simply gave the grieving relatives a pot of ash. It was a classic con which appalled many people here in Malaga.'

At the time of writing, Cubus continues to live comfortably in his luxury home, while Frank Voyce and the rest of his ex-servicemen colleagues live in dread about how they will cope with the next member's death.

CHAPTER EIGHT

MASTER CRIMINAL LENNY

Marbella, where Lenny still finances the
'occasional' drugs deal

MASTER CRIMINAL LENNY

The antics of Britain's major criminals on the Costa del Sol have had more than their fair share of coverage, but it's worth introducing you to Lenny. His story is a classic tale that shows why the sunny shores of southern Spain have attracted so much scum over the years. Forget extradition treaties and so-called amnesties: Lenny's survival on the mean streets of the Costa del Crime is testament to the bizarre lifestyle led by so many ex-pats who live on the other side of the law. How they've continued to thrive is anyone's guess.

Lenny, as he proudly says, 'floated over' to Spain in the early 1980s. His career as a reckless young armed robber on the streets of south-east London had landed him with a seven-year stretch in Parkhurst. 'By the time I'd got out I'd done a lot of thinking, and I knew I had to get out of the smoke,' says Lenny. 'A few of me old mates had bought property out on the Costa del Sol so I thought, "Why not?" I had a few bob stashed away, and the missus was up for it.'

Lenny has this habit of making everything sound very spontaneous. In truth, he knew exactly what he was doing. His main criminal financier had already told him that armed robberies were a thing of the past and drugs were now where all the money was to be earned. 'Like most villains at that time, I was strictly anti-drugs. I thought they was evil, but a man's got to earn a living somehow, and this backer said he had a hundred grand to put into a dead-cert drugs deal. So I got involved.'

Armed with his overnight bag and a Spanish dictionary, Lenny flew into Malaga and set himself up as a drugs middleman. His first £100,000 deal for a big shipment of cannabis from Morocco bought in a 500 per cent profit for Lenny's backer, and he personally skimmed a £50,000 commission. 'Back then that was good money,' says Lenny today. 'I knew what side my bread was buttered, so I reinvested that dosh in a side shipment of puff. Came out two hundred grand richer within a month. I was up and running.'

At first, Lenny insists, he only dealt in cannabis. 'I steered well clear of charley, because the Spanish Old Bill were coming down like a ton of bricks on anyone caught with the stuff. They didn't seem so bothered about puff.'

Within 18 months of arriving in Spain, Lenny was living in a plush five-bedroom villa in the mountains behind Estepona, complete with swimming pool and two Rottweilers. 'The missus was pregnant with our first kid. Life was sweet. I had the right contacts to keep pulling in the puff deals. But then some bastard went and ruined it all for me.

'I'd rented a house down near the beach for three months and we used the garage as a base to run bails of puff from the high-powered inflatable motorboats I had bringing the produce over from Morocco. It was a piece of cake. They'd drop the bails off on the beach and we'd turn up in four-by-fours and load them all up. I had half a dozen locals working for me. They got good wedge from me and seemed happy. Then it turned out the house I was renting was next door to a villa owned by a Madrid police chief. Bit of bad luck, really. The copper who took me in to Marbella nick said the only reason I got nicked was because the Madrid copper had a load of bodyguards in case of terrorist attacks and one of them had spotted what we was up to.'

It was then, according to Lenny, that he first came upon an old Spanish police tradition. 'There I was, under arrest, looking at a long stretch when a copper there, who I had never seen before and was unconnected to the case, gets up, closes the door and suggests that for fifty grand I could get released without charge. "Witnesses can go missing, señor," he says. "Files can get lost. It's easily done, but we need to come to some kind of arrangement." Well, I didn't need to hear any more. I got on to my money man, we made a delivery to that copper's Swiss bank account and, hey presto, I'm back out on the streets.'

Lenny says that, from that moment on, he made sure to have Costa del Sol police officers in his pocket so as to avoid any future 'problems'. 'It was costing me a fucking packet so I had to start bringing in shipments of the heavy stuff because the profits were much bigger.' By 'heavy stuff' Lenny was referring to cocaine and heroin. 'I was soon locked into a big-time set-up. But I treated it like a business. I kept the books very carefully. I never flashed my cash around too much because I knew I was constantly being looked at by the Spanish and British Old Bill. I had to keep my nose clean.'

By the mid-1980s, Lenny reckons he was raking in more than half a million pounds a year on drug deals alone. 'Then I started investing in property all along the coast. It was a fucking goldmine. I was living the good life but trying to keep a low profile just in case I came a cropper.'

In a desperate bid to launder his ever-increasing annual fortune, Lenny even bought himself a brothel on the outskirts of Torremolinos. 'I had to have a business to sink the money into. I got a mate to hire in the girls who used to run clubs in Soho. You know what? They said it was the happiest brothel on the Costa del Sol because I didn't care if none of the girls serviced any fellas. I just wanted them to be in the main bar supping at drinks so that when the law came in for a snoop they'd think I'd sunk all my dosh into this venture. I even paid the girls a good wedge just for being there. They'd never had it so good. You wouldn't believe the number of girls who wanted to work in that place!'

But then Lenny fell foul of the Spanish mafia and was

forced to hand the brothel over to a local family who had a monopoly on the local sex trade. 'They was right pissed off that a Brit had muscled in on what they considered to be their rightful business. Things got a bit heavy for a while. A few Molotov cocktails were chucked through my front window, if you know what I mean. In the end it was more trouble than it was worth, so I cut and run. Same Spanish fuckers are running the place to this day. It's a pity really, because all the girls were happy as pie when I was in charge.'

In the late-1980s, Lenny says he got involved in a drugs-smuggling ring headed by notorious Great Train robber Charlie Wilson. 'Charlie was a fucking smooth operator. He knew all the right people here, in the UK and in South America. It was the nearest thing to a proper criminal corporation I've ever been involved in. We all had ranks within the Firm and Charlie looked on me as one of his most trusted captains. It was a classic, old-fashioned operation.'

Soon Lenny was personally managing the smuggling of more than a million pounds' worth of drugs – cocaine, cannabis and ecstasy – every week. 'It was vast. There was more than fifty employees and I was copping fifty grand each week.'

But the good times didn't last that long. In April 1990, a criminal rival paid two hitmen to kill Charlie Wilson in the garden of his house near Marbella; the entire criminal enterprise collapsed virtually overnight. 'The British and Spanish law were all over us like flies. We couldn't move out of our homes without a shadow. It was a fucking nightmare. I'll never understand why Charlie was topped. They reckoned he'd grassed up some Amsterdam-based crim, but Charlie was renowned as a quiet man. He never talked about anyone out of turn. It just wasn't his style.'

With his vast weekly salary reduced virtually overnight to nothing, Lenny then found himself having to greasc a lot of palms to avoid being grassed up by other criminals to the police. 'It cost me a fortune. I had to sell my house just to pay off all the right fellas to avoid being nicked. It was like a house of cards tumbling down and everyone knew I'd been connected to Charlie's operation. The pressure was really being piled on me from all directions.'

For the next 18 months, Lenny kept a low profile as many of his one-time criminal associates got themselves arrested or killed. 'It was like the night of the long knives in every sense of the word. I can't deny I was scared. Every time I went out in my motor I took long-winded routes just to make sure anyone following would lose me. I never dealt in bank accounts. Everything was in cash and there wasn't much of that floating around either because I had to keep my nose completely clean.'

Eventually, Lenny used a secret nest egg of cash that he'd kept with an accountant in Gibraltar for a rainy day. 'I just had enough for a small house out in the sticks for me, the wife and our two sons. I wanted to keep well away from the action from now on. I also had enough cash left over to invest in one decent-sized puff deal.'

By this time, Spanish, British and US drug enforcement agencies were concentrating all their efforts on Class-A substances like cocaine and heroin. 'The Spanish cops were now totally uninterested in puff, but there was still a big demand for it on the Costa del Sol, so I took one big punt. It worked and I started easing myself gently back into the business.'

But by the late-1990s, the price of all drugs had plummeted so badly that Lenny started dealing in cocaine once again 'because the produce was much smaller and easier to handle'. He explained the logistics to me. 'Half a million quids' worth of charley barely fills a suitcase, while the same amount of puff requires a bloody boat for transportation. I was back in the frame but I really didn't have much choice.'

These days, Lenny is back living in a big detached house on the outskirts of Marbella, but insists that he only finances 'occasional' drug deals. 'I've learned my lesson and I try to keep one step removed from the heavy brigade these days. There's always a demand for a financial backer like me, but the art is in avoiding all direct contact with the handlers.'

Lenny is now in his early 50s. He admits he will probably never earn an honest living. 'That's just the way it is for me. I keep reading in the papers about these evil drugs barons who live it up on the Costa del Sol. Well, I can tell you, I'm one of them but I'm not a truly bad person. Is it really any worse than selling cigarettes or alcohol? I don't think so. Do you?'

CHAPTER NINE
SLAVE GIRL

Terrified Tracy Rose is still
too traumatised by her ordal to
be identified

SLAVE GIRL

For more than 20 years, British girls have been lured by the supposed good life on the Costa del Sol. Naïve youngsters all too often set out for the sunshine coast looking for fun, adventure and romance. Many even dream about settling down to a glamorous lifestyle with a glittering career a million miles away from the dole queues and freezing temperatures of the UK. But for one such girl, those dreams fell cruelly apart when she became entrapped in a den of depravity from which there was no escape. Her story should stand as a grim warning to any others planning a similar move to the Costa del Sol.

Tracey Rose's decision to turn her life around and move to southern Spain was greeted with great indifference by her family back in Luton, Bedfordshire, in the heart of Middle England. 'Why don't you get a proper job?' asked her father, just moments after 22-year-old Tracey announced she'd taken a job as a Marbella timeshare salesperson.

'I need a bit of adventure before I settle down, Dad,' replied Tracey. 'Is that such a sin?'

Her father didn't reply.

But within a couple of weeks of arriving on the Costa del Sol, the pretty university graduate began to regret her bold statement. Her job selling shares in apartments entailed a hell of a lot more persuasion of clients than Tracey had ever imagined. Some of the other girls she met working on the same job unsubtly suggested the only way to make a definite sale and earn some decent commission was to sleep with male clients.

Tracey was appalled at the prospect and, after fruitlessly trying to prove her point by getting a 'straight' sale without any sexual enticement, she quit in disgust. But the job had come with a free apartment and that meant she was now out on the streets with only a few hundred pounds in savings and a handful of phone numbers of recent friends and acquaintances.

However, Tracey's stubborn pride prevented her from returning home. She had a point to prove to her family and she was determined not to give up at the first hurdle. So she checked into a cheap hotel in the old quarter of the resort of Estepona and began looking for work. It wasn't as easy as she initially thought. She spoke no Spanish, and there had been a recent local backlash against employing anyone with an English accent. 'They said that Brits were nothing but trouble,'

Tracey later recalled. 'And in some ways I could see what they meant. Everywhere I looked were drunken Brits behaving like hooligans. No wonder we have such a bad reputation abroad.'

The following night, down on her luck and feeling very sorry for herself, Tracey arranged to meet a girlfriend from her former timeshare job for a drink in the picturesque marina area of Estepona. It was a steaming hot evening and thousands of revellers packed the narrow streets, pouring in and out of the numerous bars and clubs. Tracey's friend never showed up that night, but she enjoyed a few drinks and tried to forget all about her troubles by chatting to a charming Arabic man from one of the big yachts in the harbour.

By midnight, Tracey and her new friend, who called himself Ali, had been joined by a couple of South American girls. Tracey found them a little too forward for her liking. She reckoned they might have been high-class hookers, rumoured by many to wander in and out of the Estepona port bars looking for rich punters. But with the sangria flowing and everyone in high spirits, Tracey didn't think twice when Ali suggested all the girls might like to come aboard his yacht for a nightcap. What could possibly happen? There were three of them and only one of him, after all...

As the party stumbled up the gangplank to the vast 120-foot yacht with its whirling radar scanner and huge satellite-TV dish, Tracey took off her black stilettos after Ali said the heels might damage the wooden deck. That was the last she could remember of the evening: she woke up the next morning to find herself tied to a bed and stripped of her clothes. There was a gag across her mouth; she felt a slight breeze run across her naked body.

'I thought I was dreaming,' she later remembered. 'I shut my eyes tightly and then opened them slowly once again in the hope it was all a nightmare. But I was still there. There was a slight rocking sensation and it was only then I realised I was still on the yacht and that it was out at sea.'

At that moment two men walked into the room. One of them was the man who called himself Ali. Tracey shut her eyes tightly and listened, hoping they would think she was still asleep. The other man was an older Arab in a headdress and flowing white robes. She opened her eyes ever so slightly and noticed that he was at least 60 years of age.

Tracey prayed they'd think she was still unconscious because she needed time to work out how to get away. The two men were having a heated conversation in Arabic. Suddenly the older man began prodding Ali in the shoulder angrily. Ali then stormed out of the room. The man turned and started walking towards Tracey, smiling. 'Why you pretend to be asleep?' he asked. 'I see your eyes open.'

At first, Tracey didn't stir in the hope he would go away. The Arab sat on the edge of the bed and ran a hand slowly up the outside of her naked thigh. Tracey felt the goosebumps on her flesh start popping. 'Come on. Wake up. It's time,' said the old man. His hand stopped at the top of her thigh and he grabbed her flesh hard and squeezed. Tracey winced and her eyes snapped open angrily. He looked down at her and smiled, exposing a crooked set of yellowing teeth.

As she struggled against the ropes around her wrist and ankles, they tightened with every movement. Then the man's hand moved to her face and he ran a finger across the black silk gag and along her top lip. It tickled in a nasty kind of way. Tracey began to shake with a combination of fear and awkwardness. She couldn't talk because of the scarf gagging her. 'You're a beautiful creature,' he muttered as his eyes hungrily panned up and down her body.

Tracey began struggling even harder against the restraints. She wanted him to know she was not about to give up without a fight. But she felt horribly vulnerable, lying there naked. He pulled at her hair and then pushed her forward while he undid the gag.

Tracey spluttered for breath. 'You bastard! Let me go.' She spat the words out contemptuously. He seemed encouraged by her outburst.

'You have much energy, English girl. That's good.' Then he bent down and tried to kiss her ear. She turned and tried to bite him hard. He reacted furiously and hit her across the face with the back of his hand. 'Bitch! You pay for that...'

Three hours later, the man finally left the room. Tracey's entire face was horribly bitten and bruised. She was crying. Then the younger man from the bar, Ali, entered. He seemed genuinely concerned. 'I'm sorry if he hurt you...'

'Please, let me go,' she screamed through her tears.

'I cannot do that yet. We want you to stay for more time.'

'You'll have to kill me first,' Tracey told Ali defiantly.

He sat down at the end of the bed and quietly told her that her drinks had been deliberately drugged earlier in the bar. She was now their prisoner. 'You'll survive if you co-operate, and you will be paid well.'

'I don't want your money. Just take me back to the shore, please,' begged Tracey, but she knew in her heart of hearts that it wasn't going to happen. She was being held captive and they could do whatever they liked to her.

Later that day, the older Arab returned and carried out another horrible sexual assault on her. As he lay on top of her, Tracey turned her head to one side, sobbed quietly and prayed that it would all end soon. 'I wanted to die at that moment,' she later recalled. 'There seemed no other means of escape.'

Tracey Rose's ordeal went on for three more agonising days. At times she tried to fight back, but she eventually became resigned to her fate, acknowledging that it was probably the key to her survival. Eventually the old Arab grew bored of her and she was dropped back at Estepona port. Ali gave her €5,000. She tried to throw it back at him, but he said, 'Take it. It'll help you. It's tough out there.'

'I'm not a prostitute,' she screamed at him. 'I don't sleep with men for money.'

'That's unimportant,' said Ali. 'If you don't take the money he'll want you back again.'

Tracey hated herself for it, but she kept the cash. She felt that Ali did have some sympathy for her. She went back to her hotel that day, showered, cried, ate and then cried again. She even tried to burn the notes but had to stop when the smoke set off a fire alarm. 'I hated myself even more than I hated them. But I didn't know what to do, or who to tell,' she explained.

Tracey eventually found herself a 'normal' job as a barmaid 30 miles east of Estepona. 'I wanted to get as far away from there as possible,' she later recalled. She still has slight scars on her wrists where the ropes burned through her skin and admits that's she's unlikely ever to recover fully from her horrific ordeal.

Then, almost six months after the appalling assault, Tracey got a painful reminder of what had happened. 'I bumped into those same two South American girls who were with me when that man Ali drugged my drink. They even asked how I was, although they made no reference to what had happened. I was astounded. It was almost as if they just thought it was no big deal. Of course, I don't know for certain that those girls were involved in my kidnap, but I think they must have known what had happened, surely?

'But you know what one of them said to me? She dropped a hint that I could earn some big money if I wanted to be a prostitute on the side. "You'd earn a lot of money because the Arabs love English girls like you." I looked completely aghast at them and ran off in tears.

I just don't know how they could be so heartless. Maybe they'd just become hardened to it all because of how they earned a living. I actually feel very sorry for girls like that because they've lost all compassion and self-respect. It's as if it's been beaten out of them. It's a terrible way to end up, isn't it?'

These days, Tracey says she's enjoying a simple existence working hard in the bar. 'I'm saving as much money as possible so I can get home in time for my granny's seventieth birthday next year. In some ways I don't know why I stayed on here in Spain after what happened, but I wanted to prove to myself that I could handle it. My parents would be so shocked if I told them, but I never will.

'It's strange the way things have turned out. Those three or four days on the yacht were a living nightmare I shall never forget, and that awful experience numbed me about everything else. I just don't think about the same sort of things any more. I have a life to live. I suppose I'm lucky I never became a prostitute. It must be so easy to just think, "What the hell," after going through something like that.

'It seems to me that there are only two types of people in this world – the givers and the takers. No wonder those girls don't give a damn about anyone but themselves...'

CHAPTER TEN

CHAIN OF EVIL

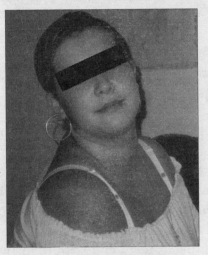

One of the vice girls involved in
the vile trade of young women

CHAIN OF EVIL

Mafia-style gangs based on the Costa del Sol have been using Bosnia as a marketplace for girls, many of whom are smuggled into Spain and then forced into a life of prostitution. My investigations along the Spanish coastline have uncovered links between crooked officials in Bosnia and a network of sex slaves organised by major criminals, including Britons, in Spain.

Over the past two years, a notorious Glasgow villain known on the Costa del Sol as 'Jimmy' has made a small fortune importing women as sex slaves from Bosnia after greasing the palms of certain members of international organisations. Jimmy boasted to me recently, 'Bosnia's in chaos, and Spain has more brothels then just about any other country in Europe, so it's an obvious destination for these girls. They have a better life over here than they would ever have back in Bosnia.'

But it's the international connection that really worries Spanish police, and European politicians and peacekeepers alike. As one UN official explained, 'We're supposed to be cracking down on the sex-slave trade and the suffering of these people, not watching it being encouraged.'

Girls as young as 15 have been illegally shipped out of Bosnia and forced to work as prostitutes on the Costa del Sol. But Jimmy, a former Glagow hardman, denies any of the girls he 'handles' are underage and he is immensely proud of his international connections. He claims that international personnel have been involved in the vice business since as far back as the mid-1990s. 'These fellas in Bosnia used the brothels there from the moment they moved in. A couple of them got caught in what you'd call compromising situations, and now they're in the pocket of the local mafia. They've got them by the goolies, which means no one will stop these girls being shipped out to Spain.'

In late 2000, a female human-rights investigator was fired shortly after trying to expose the Bosnian vice ring. Kathryn Bolkovac claimed that women were forced to dance naked in Bosnian bars frequented by UN police officers. Her account turned out to be the tip of the iceberg: it has now emerged that some officials had already forged links with the local mafia, and they've been making vast sums of cash by 'nodding through' shiploads of girls travelling out of Bosnia.

As one of Jimmy's associates, a south Londoner called Terry, told me, 'Jimmy can get whatever he wants in

Bosnia. They provide a guarantee for the girls to get out of Bosnia in the first place.'

At one Costa del Sol brothel near Malaga Airport, a Bosnian teenager called Naomi, who claims to be 18, openly admits how she was brought to Spain. 'The travel documents were obtained through a man who owns a nightclub near my home in Bosnia. Then they handed me over to this British guy and he brought me to this place. I cannot leave for at least six months until I've paid off my airfare and rent to stay here. I need to earn a lot of money to send back to my family and to pay for me to go to university.'

Naomi's brunette friend Julia, 19, says she hates working in the brothel and wants to go back to her family in Bosnia. 'But they've trapped me here until I've paid off all my debts. It disgusts me to go with these men, but I have no choice.'

Both girls blame the international organisations for their predicament. 'They are no better than the local police. They come into our country to give us peace, but instead we end up being forced to have sex with men in a foreign country away from our families. We hate them,' says Naomi.

One of the alleged middlemen between the crooked officials in Bosnia and the criminals of the Costa del Sol is another Briton called Patrick. He is also proud of his connections with the international organisations. 'They're cool guys. They know what the score is and that prostitution is no big deal here in Spain or over in Bosnia. The girls earn good money, so what's the problem?'

Others might disagree. Señor Jorge Santiago of the Costa del Sol's *Guardia Civil* police force says, 'These men are involved in smuggling women to Spain, many against their will. There is no other way to describe it. The brothel keepers are encouraging some bad people to make money out of the misery of women. It disgusts me.'

Bosnia itself is full of so-called 'girly bars' frequented by UN policemen. 'These places are like a showcase for the girls. When they're spotted, they are forced to work as prostitutes abroad,' says one visitor to Bosnia.

In December 2000, Kathryn Bolkovac sent an email to Jacques Paul Klein, the chief of the UN mission in Bosnia and Herzegovina, highlighting the sexual exploitation of women by those who had been sent to protect them from the sex trade in the first place. Mrs Bolkovac also claimed that many women and underage girls were handed over to bar owners and told to perform sex acts to pay for their costumes in those brothels and bars. But even worse, Mrs Bolkovac stated, 'The women who refused were locked in rooms and withheld food and outside contact for days or weeks. After this time they were told to dance naked on tabletops and sit with clients. If the women still refused to perform sex acts with the customers they are beaten and raped in the rooms by the bar owners and their associates. They're told if they go to the police they will be arrested for prostitution and being an illegal immigrant.'

Back in the Costa del Sol, sex-slave trafficker Jimmy claims he has paid thousands of pounds in bribes for officials to issue travel documents to the girls so that they can be shipped out to Spain and a life of vice. 'Having international organisations running things over there is perfect for us because then things get done real quick.'

Meanwhile, Naomi and Julia at the brothel near Malaga Airport continue working from 6pm to 6am, servicing up to ten men a night. 'I want to go back to my family but the men here say that I have to first earn the money to pay for my crossing and papers through the international organisations,' says Julia. 'We are always being told how good they are for us. Well, try telling that to the Bosnian girls who've ended up in these brothels.'

Yet despite all the evidence, some senior UN officials still continue to play down the situation. One spokesman for the UN High Commissioner for Refugees said recently, 'I don't think anyone should be too surprised that out of many thousands of international personnel a bunch of them should get up to naughty tricks. It happens in every war – it's just sad that they are wearing blue berets.'

One senior Bosnian policeman summed up the situation when he said, 'This is a pitiful thing. It is a pitiful life. You should tell the world we never lived like this before, and I hope we never will again.'

But as Jimmy explained, 'There will always be someone prepared to take a bribe, and there's always a load of men who want sex with these girls. I call it supply and demand.'

CHAPTER ELEVEN

ARTFUL JOHN

Many of John Green's Lowry
fakes were sold in top Marbella
clubs and bars

ARTFUL JOHN

John Green squinted closely at the canvas in the Spanish sunlight and then added a dab or two of paint before turning towards me and saying, 'Lowrys are a piece of cake to copy. There are thousands in circulation and most of them sail past the so-called experts.'

But then Green, the most prolific forger since the notorious Tom Keating, always did love the thrill of conning the art world as much as he enjoyed the fruits of his ill-gotten gains. His masterstrokes made him king of the great Lowry-lookalike industry, and the safest place for him was always going to be the Costa del Crime. Then, one day, he mysteriously disappeared. Some people believe he may have paid the ultimate price for humiliating some of the heaviest faces in the British underworld community of southern Spain. Others reckon the old rogue has slipped the police net to set up home in the mountains behind Estepona with one of his numerous Latino girlfriends.

But wherever he is, John Green, now in his early 70s, would have been greatly amused by a recent, much-hyped auction of Lowry paintings at Sotheby's. 'He'd have loved to think that one or two of his fakes were in there amongst the genuine Lowrys,' says one old Estepona friend called Mitch.

Many of the 30 Lowrys up for grabs at Sotheby's went for between £250,000 and £400,000. John Green's legendary output of forgeries never sold for those sort of prices, but he still managed to make a good living in Spain out of paintings that he saw as the ultimate humiliation of the art establishment.

Over the years, numerous Green Lowrys found their way into London's top auction houses. Most were eventually spotted, but at least a dozen are believed to have slipped through the net. Many of those now hang in places of honour in private houses. Most fakes only come to light after the death of their purchaser.

Eccentric Manchester rent collector LS Lowry, whose tiny stick figures in bleak industrial townscapes made him one of the world's most instantly recognised artists, died in 1976. But thanks to John Green and a handful of others, he is currently one of the most forged artists in the world.

'I enjoy painting, so why not make a few bob out of it at the same time?' Green asked me when I encountered him in Spain before he disappeared. 'If people are stupid enough to think these are real Lowrys, they deserve everything they get.'

The biggest nightmare for experts is that Lowry himself never properly recorded his output. In a working life that spanned almost three quarters of a century, the best estimate is that Lowry produced about a thousand paintings and eight to nine thousand drawings. But this is no more than a well-informed guess. 'That's why it's been so easy for me to get away with forging him,' added Green, who was at the time living in a charming little beachside urbanisation a few miles west of Estepona.

Back in London, art dealers even begrudgingly admired the work of Green compared to other forgers. 'Their quality ranges from quite dreadful to rather impressive,' says one dealer. 'Green's efforts are actually in the top ten per cent.'

Green's recent disappearance from his old haunts on the Costa del Sol may have been prompted when Lowry's rare London scene of Piccadilly Circus (virtually all his other paintings depicted the north of England) comfortably broke the previous Lowry price record when it sold for £562,500 in London in 2000. Over on the Costa del Crime, gregarious John Green rubbed his hands with glee and decided to quadruple the price of his forgeries virtually overnight. 'That's when things started to get pretty hairy for John,' says his old Costa del Sol crony Mitch. 'He got greedy and sold about half a dozen Lowrys for at least £40,000 each. God knows what those punters thought when they discovered they'd been fleeced.'

John Green had a number of regular customers whom he met while hanging out in some of Marbella's priciest bars and bridge clubs. 'John thought it was a right laugh to con these people. I told him to be careful, but he's the most reckless man I've ever met,' added Mitch.

As another of Green's Costa del Sol acquaintances explained, 'Some of these people were retired bank robbers and big-time drug barons. People you shouldn't mess with.' A few years earlier Green had proudly boasted that one of his most famous customers was Great Train robber Charlie Wilson. Wilson was murdered by a hitman in the garden of his Costa del Sol villa in 1990.

It's all a far cry from Brackley, Northamptonshire, where John Green ran an electrical business and took a few painting lessons at night school after his family told him he had a natural talent as an artist. Green first began copying Lowry after a bet with a friend following a visit to a Lowry exhibition in London in 1970. 'I said I didn't think they were any good,' he later explained, 'so my friend bet me that I couldn't copy his style.' Green took him up on the bet and was surprised at the ease with which he sold the painting in Paris for £1,500. 'That got me thinking and I soon got hooked.'

Green eventually became so confident of his abilities as a forger that he also began copying the works of other artists such as French Impressionists Monet and Manet, as well as English masters like Constable. He even turned his hand to modern British artist Helen Bradley.

After Lowry's death in 1976, Green stepped up his output of fakes. Within two years, dozens of previously unknown pictures were advertised for sale in UK national newspapers as the property of a private collector called Mr Gilbert – aka John Green. 'Mr Gilbert' flogged off the paintings for way below the market value at the time. Back then, the highest price for a genuine Lowry was no more than £20,000. 'I made a few grand each time. There's no harm in that,' Green told me during our interview on the Costa del Sol.

One of Green's early favourites was entitled *Man with Walking Stick in Street* and, much to the forger's delight, his version even found its way into the Christie's catalogue for their sale of modern pictures in the autumn of 1980. John Green had proudly recreated the drawing from a book called *Drawings of LS Lowry*, which was published in 1963. He had photocopied the picture in the book and then worked over the photocopy with pencil until it was what he thought was an exact replica. Christie's hastily withdrew the sketch after one of Lowry's oldest friends contacted them to say it couldn't be genuine because he owned the original.

Besides replicating certain classic Lowrys, Green was also a deft hand at constructing new pictures by copying portions of genuine Lowrys and merging them into fresh Lowry-type scenes. 'Those are the ones I try to charge the most for because there's a good chance no one will ever work out if they're fake,' Green explained to me.

But why, I asked Green, didn't he just stick to doing the 'brand-new' pictures? 'I consider forging actual paintings to be a real skill, so the ultimate challenge for me is to recreate an exact replica of an existing painting. I just can't resist doing them.'

Back in 1982, Green skipped bail and headed off to sunny Spain after Scotland Yard's art and antiques squad had arrested and charged him with three specimen offences of criminal deception totalling £11,350 following complaints from two of his victims. Then detectives traced another 14 fake Lowrys; further information indicated Green had sold at least another 28 forgeries to unsuspecting art lovers. Even Detective Sergeant Paul Fowlie, who had arrested Green, conceded he had a sneaking admiration for the runaway forger. 'I've always been convinced that he started painting fakes for the thrill of it. He enjoyed taking the risks.'

Green was immensely proud of the studio in the loft of his Spanish villa near Estepona. It was filled with canvas, paints, brushes and the most important tools of his trade – art books containing photos of the paintings he so slavishly forged. Green himself even claimed to have met Lowry in 1970, six years before the famous artist's death. 'If only he'd known what I'd get up to.' He also claimed to own three genuine Lowrys. 'They're vital for me because they provide me with invaluable proof of Lowry's techniques.'

Green, who took about a week to knock out each fake, always ensured his forgeries came with battered-looking frames. So how do you know in a glance whether your Lowry is the real thing or a John Green edition? 'One of Lowry's trademarks was his use of a white background.

But he used to "age" that for years before laying it on the canvas and starting the actual painting,' explains one real expert. 'So in genuine examples it isn't white at all, but a subtle creamy shade. Forgers haven't the time or the patience for that.'

However, just like the late Tom Keating, whose forgeries now fetch high prices themselves, Green relished duping dealers and the foolish rich to feed his hedonistic lifestyle on the Costa del Sol. 'Sometimes I advertise a bunch of paintings in newspapers, claiming they're part of an unwanted legacy,' Green told me when we met. 'Then I slip in one of my Lowrys amongst the rubbish that I've bought cheaply. Dealers came along and look through the collection and it's great to see those mugs' eyes pop out when they find the Lowry. Of course, they'd never tell me what they'd found and they'd pay a few thousand pounds thinking they'd just got a bargain.'

The Phillips auction house in London estimates that three in every ten supposed Lowrys brought to them are fakes. But then Phillips know all about John Green. A few years back they unknowingly sold a Green Lowry as the real thing. Glasgow-based father-and-son businessmen William and Graeme Baxter met Green at a bridge club in Marbella in the mid-1980s and agreed to take one of his Lowrys to the big London auction houses in exchange for 10 per cent commission. They had no idea it was a forgery. The auction house eventually accepted the painting and it sold for £4,800 after Green had furnished them with some 'background history' of the painting. He claimed the painting, of a northern industrial scene, had been bought by his late father, Dr JF Gilbert from Alderly Edge, Cheshire, and had been left to him in his will.

Green was so pleased with the sale that he immediately sent over another Lowry. But it was quickly identified by the auctioneers as a fake. The original painting which sold was then recalled and the Baxters were forced to pay the purchaser back his £4,800.

Graeme Baxter was so furious he flew out to Spain to confront Green, but he was nowhere to be found. His father William later explained, 'This whole business was shattering. Green is a rogue and if I get hold of him I'd like to strangle him.'

But while the Baxters gave up on Green, others did not. According to one of Green's oldest cronies on the Costa del Sol, the crafty forger first did a disappearing act after a private detective turned up at his Estepona home and demanded his client's money back 'with menaces'.

Around the same time, one London businessman who bought a Green Lowry for £10,000 claims he was approached by a 'criminal type' from the bridge-and-gin-and-tonic brigade in Marbella. 'He asked me if I'd put some money in a pot to give Green the sort of scare that might make him pay us our money back,' said the businessman, too embarrassed to be identified. 'But I'm not into that sort of behaviour, although I still want my money back and he should be properly dealt with by the authorities.'

Green's Estepona friend Justin Ketch explained,

'There was a price on John's head. No doubt about it. He had to get out of here in a hurry.' Manuel Pintes, the owner of a bar just a couple of hundred yards from Green's Estepona villa, wasn't surprised when Green did his midnight flit. 'John always pushed his luck. If it wasn't problems caused by his forgeries then it was some girlfriend or other kicking him out of the house.'

Green openly boasted to his friends on the Costa del Sol that he believed he had the right to con the British villains he encountered to 'give them a taste of their own medicine'. But now it seems that some of those 'mugs' whom John Green so obsessively hoaxed may have committed the ultimate act of revenge. 'Either that or he's laughing at us from some pretty little *finca* up in the mountains,' said one of his old Costa del Sol friends.

CHAPTER TWELVE
HITMAN LUIS

An executioner's wage pays for a comfortable home in the hills around Marbella

HITMAN LUIS

There is plenty of work for a good hitman on the Costa del Sol. The number of shootists on the streets of southern Spain has reached almost epidemic proportions in recent times. Twenty years ago, if you wanted someone bumped off there were only a handful of highly professional killers-for-hire available. But in 2003 there were more than a hundred acknowledged hits on the Costa del Sol – and they are just the ones the Spanish police know about. Many of these professional hits get little or no newspaper coverage. As one British journalist based in Spain says, 'One villain knocking off another doesn't have the same news appeal as a beautiful brunette blasting her cheating husband to death.'

Not surprisingly, hitmen on the Costa del Crime tend to keep a low profile. Says one, 'The less publicity the better. Luckily the papers don't seem that interested in most hits, and that's the way we like it.'

But the Spanish police admit the situation has now spiralled totally out of control. One detective based in Marbella told me, 'Drugs have brought with them many hitmen. Some of these criminals would commission a contract killer for the smallest reason. It's a very dangerous situation.'

The bottom line is that life is a lot cheaper in 21st-century Spain than it was when armed robbers brandishing sawn-off shotguns swaggered across pavements in south London taking pot-shots at anyone in their way. These days, there are numerous small-time hoods prepared to knock off other villains, cheating lovers or work rivals, which could eventually put the real pros out of business.

Take 'Luis'. He's half-Spanish, half-English and has been in 'the business' for 12 years. He lives in a big pad in the hills behind Malaga, and no one other than his dear old mum, his wife and his kids knows his real identity. That's the way he intends to keep it. 'I do the job clean and simple, with no fucking aggro,' explains Luis. 'That's why people come to me when they have a problem.'

Luis reckons the hired hand who popped a French couple on a quiet street in Marbella a couple of years back didn't put a foot wrong. The married pair were iced as part of a turf war between drug dealers and brothel owners in the area. 'I heard it cost £20,000 each person, which is a good deal for everyone concerned.' The couple were shot at point-blank range outside their modern detached home only a few hundred yards from the local police station. They had been telling people there was 'a bullet out there with our names on it' because they'd turned police informants. The drugs ring they were connected to had links to an American mafia branch in Detroit, not to mention a number of men from Medellin in Colombia. So when they finally got rubbed out on their own doorstep at 1am, there wasn't a lot of grieving.

The Marbella police didn't have anyone in the frame and made it clear they weren't that bothered about the killing. It turned out that the couple had double-crossed numerous criminal associates, ripped off call girls and hugely upset certain cocaine dealers. Some poor mug had even bought a second-hand car off them and discovered it was hot.

Luis himself is renowned as one of the most feared shootists in southern Spain. 'The rules of the game are changing every day. My basic price is €30,000, unless I'm being asked to take out a big-time criminal who's got a lot of protection. I always get paid in full, in advance, in cash. How else could I handle it, take a cheque? There are other unwritten clauses that go into every hit contract. If I get arrested, the person commissioning the hit takes care of all my legal costs plus my bail if I manage to get it. He'd also make sure I was comfortable in prison, that my wife was comfortable at home, as well as do everything to try and get me out. Finally, when I finish my sentence, he would have a bundle of cash waiting for me. This is done to guarantee silence. As long as all obligations are taken care of, I'm not going to say a word to no one. I'm certainly not going to land anyone in the shit. They'd soon finish me off.'

But Luis says it's not the risk of being caught for his crimes that bothers him. 'There are other so-called pros out there killing people for €5,000 each job. But you get what you pay for and these cut-price operators all get caught in the end and then they start singing to the police. Let's face it, a grandmother in Benalmadena who wants her husband killed after thirty years of abuse is going to end up hiring an amateur or an undercover policeman. There's too many small-time hoods making out they can carry out hits for next to nothing. All they do is make problems for people like me.'

But Luis thinks he knows exactly what the future holds for him. 'I'm planning to retire soon. Buy myself a nice little villa in northern Spain and start relaxing and enjoying my life.' He pauses and nods his head slowly. 'If I live that long...'

CHAPTER THIRTEEN
SLIPPERY JOE

Joe Wilkins – slippery
when wanted

SLIPPERY JOE

Joe Wilkins was one of a dying breed of Costa del Sol criminals. He loved playing everyone off against each other: the cops, other mobsters, even poor old Joe Public. They've all provided an income to artful Joe Wilkins.

When one of Scotland Yard's most disastrous stings came crashing down leaving London's police with a £25 million bill after a court case against a suspected money-laundering gang collapsed in the summer of 2003, guess who was being blamed? Old Joe Wilkins. He undoubtedly played a pivotal role in the operation despite being an escaped convict, sometime fraudster, Soho vice king and friend to many of Britain and Spain's most notorious gangsters. Scotland Yard detectives had set up an operation to catch drugs and tobacco smugglers based in Spain and Gibraltar, using Joe Wilkins to introduce them to the major players. But what on earth were the Old Bill doing using a dodgepot like Wilkins as a supposedly reliable police informer?

This bizarre tale kicked off in 1992 when Wilkins went on the run from a low-security prison in East Anglia where he was serving ten years for drugs smuggling. Like so many others, he turned up a few months later on the Costa del Crime where he got tapped by undercover detectives who wanted his help setting up the sting. Wilkins, well-connected in the British underworld community, was encouraged to introduce coppers posing as dodgy businessmen to major villains operating in Spain and Gibraltar. They were lured into investing their dirty money into a laundering scheme that was really a police front. It turned into a five-year operation that ensnared dozens of criminals who were laundering money from drugs, tobacco and vice rackets. But that sting eventually ended up causing years of legal wrangling and accusations of entrapment against the long arm of the law.

In August 2003, the main case against ten men was thrown out at London's Southwark Crown Court after 414 days in court, with the judge denouncing the sting as 'massively illegal'. But then Joe Wilkins, whose Houdini-like ability to evade jail has caused the underworld to suspect him of being an MI6 and police informant, was never one to do things by halves. This south Londoner with more front than Woolworths is rumoured to have played a role in the 1988 Gibraltar shootings in which three IRA members were gunned down by the SAS in cold blood. It is also rumoured that he was given a helping hand to flee prison so that he could specifically move to Spain and work as a major informer for the Old Bill, who've long been obsessed with nicking many of the villains still languishing in luxury on the Costa del Crime.

At 6 feet 3 inches tall, Joe Wilkins was a handsome, larger-than-life character who favoured Michael Caine-style glasses and was even married for a time to the glamorous dancer Pearl Read who later modelled at the age of 56 in her bra as part of Age Concern's 1998 advertising poster campaign. Back in 1972, Wilkins had been at the centre of the Soho turf wars, and was even shot at in his office by a rival gangster. He took two bullets in the chest but survived. In August 1987, British Customs intercepted a fishing boat called *Danny Boy* off the Sussex coast. On board were 30 sacks of Moroccan hashish worth £1.5 million. Joe Wilkins and several other men were nicked. He was eventually jailed for ten years for being the 'heart and centre' of the plot.

It was then that Wilkins's life story took its strangest twist. Despite his long criminal background, Wilkins was transferred to Ford open prison in Sussex soon after being sentenced. While in prison, he became involved in controversy over the 1989 Thames Television programme *Death on the Rock* about the SAS shootings in Gibraltar. A local woman, Carmen Proetta, who saw the shooting from her window, was one of those who challenged the official account. Wilkins claimed to the *Sunday Times* that he could discredit Mrs Proetta. The newspaper's lawyer took a statement from him in prison. In return, Wilkins wanted money. The *Sunday Times* paid Wilkins's sister £2,000; but his claims about Mrs Proetta were later shown to be false.

In 1991, Wilkins walked out of Ford only to be rearrested and taken to Highpoint low-security prison. In January 1992, he was allowed out on an unaccompanied visit to his dentist in London, and fled to Spain. He was soon living openly in a villa in Estepona, slap bang in the middle of the Costa del Crime world of drugs smuggling and money laundering.

It is alleged that Wilkins then became an agent provocateur in the discredited police operation in Gibraltar. In the early-1990s, the Foreign Office had become concerned over allegations that senior politicians in Gibraltar were involved with lucrative drugs- and tobacco-smuggling operations. Wilkins is said to have helped with the top-secret sting, making introductions and identifying leading smugglers. But no arrests were ever made.

About the same time, an experienced Scotland Yard undercover officer suggested using the American technique of a 'reverse sting', in which the police set up a money-laundering front to reel in well-known criminals. The British version was codenamed Operation Cotton, and the first task of the undercover officer was to go to Spain and meet Joe Wilkins, who introduced him to Christopher Finch, 55, a leading lawyer in Gibraltar. Finch had been the Thames Television lawyer during the making of the *Death on the Rock* programme. In turn, Finch introduced the undercover cop to Plinio Bossino, 66, who ran *bureau de change* outlets in Gibraltar. What was said at those early meetings is now disputed, as the tapes of the conversation have been lost by Scotland Yard. Finch and Bossino solicited their criminal contacts to launder money through what appeared to be a Mayfair-based financial services company but which, in reality, was the front for the police sting. Dozens of people were eventually arrested.

It was at the Southwark Crown Court trial in the summer of 2003 that Judge George Bathurst Norman described the operation as 'massively illegal' because British law does not allow entrapment. He ruled that Finch had been entrapped but Bossino had not. Charges against all the defendants were eventually dropped.

Wilkins was even rumoured to have informed on master criminal Kenneth Noye, who went on the run after the 1996 M25 road-rage murder of Stephen Cameron. It is even said that Noye stayed at Wilkins's villa. He was arrested shortly afterwards near Cadiz. But as one Costa del Sol source told me, 'It would take a mighty brave man to grass up Noye and I don't think Joe would have done it.'

In his later years, Wilkins became *persona non grata* with the highly paranoid British criminal fraternity in Spain. A well-informed British underworld source in Spain told me, 'If Joe was helping the spooks [MI6], that may explain why it was so easy for him to go on his toes [escape from prison] and why he lived so openly. The view is taken here that he was a grass.'

Wilkins spent the rest of his life on the Costa del Crime. When questions were asked in parliament about why Joe Wilkins had not been extradited or deported from Spain, the Home Office consistently refused to comment.

CHAPTER FOURTEEN

GIRLS' NIGHT OUT

The assistant to Mayor Checa

GIRLS' NIGHT OUT

It's not just murder, sex and mayhem on the Costa del Sol. This is the story of how a town full of long-suffering Costa del Sol wives hit back and created the ultimate girls' night out – once a week. All the men in their entire town just inland from many of southern Spain's most notorious resorts have been barred from going out after dark. And the town's Mayor has even started fining them if they break the curfew because he wants to encourage men to stay at home every Thursday night to look after their children and clean their homes while their wives are given a free run of the town's bars and nightclubs.

'It might sound like a joke, but it's deadly serious and we're all determined to have a good time while our husbands are at home doing the cleaning and looking after the family,' laughed one housewife as she toasted the new law that has given the womenfolk of the town a streak of independence they never realised existed.

Javier Checa, Mayor of the Spanish town of Torredonjimeno (population 14,000), has created a law that bans men from the streets between 9pm and 2am. He believes many towns on the Costa del Sol will soon follow suit. Money from the fines imposed by Mayor Checa's specially recruited team of women 'enforcement officers' is being put towards groups that deal with domestic violence and equality between the sexes. It is estimated that a quarter of all wives in Spain suffer some form of violence from their husbands. One expert explained, 'Until recently, these incidents were rarely spoken about let alone prosecuted, and anything that helps bring this subject out in the open is important.'

Says Mayor Checa, 'We have to make men aware of the responsibilities they have in the home. They don't just have a right to go out and drink beer with their friends, they also have to be a house husband.'

The Mayor even wants to encourage more Brits and other northern Europeans to move into his town because 'they have more respect for women and we can learn from them.' He also believes it is essential that other towns on the Costa del Sol introduce similar laws. 'I know that quite a few mayors along the coast are watching my scheme closely, so who knows which towns will adopt this next?'

Local council chief Maria Teresa Castellano, 36, fully supports the Mayor's new law. 'The Mayor is highlighting a very serious problem and should be congratulated. I fully support this move. Spanish men have been allowed to believe they were in charge for too long. It is time they learned the truth about today's world.'

But some of the men of Torredonjimeno are angry with the Mayor's new ruling. Farmer José Luis Jimenez says, 'I don't see that the Mayor can tell us when we should be able to go out for a beer. We have the right to do that if and when we want. He should mind his own business.'

Mayor Checa started his male-free zone in the summer of 2003 and christened it 'The Night of the Women' in recognition of Spain's domestic-violence problem. Checa believes his initiative has fractured Spain's traditional social norms and helped give a lifeline to many of the town's female population, who have been under the thumb of their domineering husbands for centuries. Now every Thursday evening as the church bell tolls 9pm, at least half a dozen of Checa's so-called 'angels' dressed like airline stewardesses start their patrols on the streets, carrying thick books of €3 tickets. The angels – led by beautiful brunette Lula Cobo – then spend five hours on the narrow lanes of Torredonjimeno enforcing this bizarre new law. 'It's a great law, which I am proud to enforce,' explains 23-year-old Lula. 'The men of this town have had it all their own way for too long and now it is the turn of the women to have a good time.'

Housewife Christabel Argnos, 31, and her best friend Beatriz Gunez, 33, say they now always make a point of going out together on Thursday nights. 'It's a great law with a serious message for all the men of Spain who still live in the past,' says Christabel. 'Women have a right to go out and enjoy themselves as well. This is an old farming community and a lot of men still believe that a woman's place is in the home. They cannot understand or accept that we have rights as well.'

Some local men have tried to beat the ban by pretending that they are foreign or from other areas of Spain whenever they're stopped by the 'angels'. But Lula and her team of enforcers are well aware of their tricks. 'We always insist they show us their identity cards, which show their home addresses. We are determined to enforce this law because it is very important.'

Local businessman Paco Estrada found himself cornered by three of Mayor Checa's angels and immediately paid his on-the-spot fine on a recent Thursday night. 'This is a good law and I will remember never to go out in the town on a Thursday night in the future.'

Meanwhile, Mayor Checa insists that the girls' night out underpins a very serious message. 'In Spain, only ten per cent of women work outside the home. Domestic violence is a huge problem. In this town alone, 142 women made complaints to the police about maltreatment – imagine how many didn't. Nobody has ever spoken about women's equality here before. Now there is a debate, thanks to the curfew.' He says what he'd really like to do is send every man who breaks the curfew to prison. 'But unfortunately the Spanish constitution does not allow that, so I have styled the fine as a "conscious donation".'

But not all women are in favour of the curfew. Teresa

Jimenez, director of the local Women's Insititute, says, 'It is a retrograde step which, far from educating men about sharing responsibilities, helps to turn the notion of equality into a joke.'

But many of the women of Torredonjimeno wholeheartedly support the Mayor's brave step. Housewife Maria Fuentes says, 'What's the big deal? We're all having a great time on Thursday nights now. And for the first time in my marriage, my husband José has even laid the dinner table and washed the dishes. Is that so bad?'

CHAPTER FIFTEEN

ROCK OF CRIME

It's criminally easy to get to
Gibraltar from the Costa del Sol

ROCK OF CRIME

At 8.30pm, with the setting sun dipping below the sheer eastern cliff of the Rock of Gibraltar, a powerful inflatable surges through the waves. Trailing a worm of phosphoresce from its outboard, the purring craft – the Spanish call them *planeadoras* – loses speed and sashays slowly into the Caleta bay just as another smaller speedboat appears, drawing foamy coils in the sea. A man in the inflatable throws at least a dozen watertight boxes into the other, smaller boat. The boxes, though bulky, are plainly not heavy.

The smaller boat then surges off towards the beach where three other men pull the craft onto the sand and quickly load the boxes into a waiting van. Out in the bay, the inflatable's powerful engine thrusts into life as it heads back across the Straits of Gibraltar towards Morocco where another consignment of cocaine awaits collection.

Welcome to the Costa del Crime's classic drugs route. The Rock is now used as a junction for hash from Morocco and cocaine from the cartel in Columbia by many of Britain's most powerful criminals. It is believed that Gibraltar's super-busy drug barons are importing more than a billion pounds' worth of narcotics each year right under the noses of officials on this little piece of Britain in the Mediterranean.

Getting in and out of the Rock is so easy for many British criminals that they've helped turn Gibraltar into the money-laundering centre of the Mediterranean; it is a virtually lawless society built around a rapidly depleted Navy whose members spend more time brawling in seedy bars than defending queen and country. Top of the list of villains who have popped in and out of the Rock in recent years is master criminal Kenneth Noye. While on the run from British police for murdering a motorist in a road-rage attack in Kent in 1996, Noye spent many months on the Rock setting up drug deals and buying cheap electrical appliances for his home in a deserted Spanish retreat, 70 miles up the road.

Noye boasted to one criminal associate that he'd never once been asked even to show the photograph in his false British passport during his numerous trips in and out of Gibraltar between 1996 and 1998. 'Kenny was told to never drive a car onto the Rock because that would be more likely to be stopped and searched, so he'd walk through the border checkpoint waving his UK passport without even having to show it,' one of Noye's associates told me.

Noye also reckoned Gibraltar was one of the easiest places to fly back into Britain from when he had deals to do and people to see back in his old manors of south-east London and Kent. But even more disturbingly, he managed to set up a number of multi-million-pound drug deals during a series of meetings with one of the Rock's most powerful drug barons. 'Those meetings on the Rock were an open secret. We all knew who Noye was, but the man he met runs the Rock and no one would dare upset him,' says one local criminal, who visited Noye on a number of occasions while he was on the run in Spain back in the late-1990s.

Kenny Noye also knew from the days back when he handled more than £20 million worth of gold bullion from the notorious Brinks Mat robbery at Heathrow in 1983 that he could convert currency into gold with ease in Gibraltar. But Noye's dodgy dealings on the Rock are only the tip of the iceberg. Gibraltar is awash with more gangsters per square mile than Chicago in the 1930s.

Thin Phil – a pseudonym, but his real first name is every bit as clichéd – is a typical member of the Gibraltar mafia. He works as a runner for a major former north-London drug baron now based on the Rock. Thin Phil and other runners can make up to £5,000 a week steering their inflatables across the ocean. His boss has numerous boats and crews, lock-ups to store drugs and dozens of people to load and unload his narcotics on both sides of the Straits.

The biggest earner used to be the hash available 14 miles due south in Morocco. It's a rich harvest of drugs less than an hour across a busy but underpoliced stretch of water. These days, however, that flotilla of speedboats and inflatables smuggles an even more valuable commodity – cocaine. The biggest irony of all this is that, while the British-run colony seems to be virtually turning a blind eye to these multi-million-pound criminal enterprises, it is 'the fucking Spanish' (as Thin Phil calls them) who are genuinely trying to crack down on this evil trade.

Spanish police now use a powerful launch – the smugglers call it a turbo – to pursue the drugs couriers in their inflatables. And, naturally, they insist that Gibraltar's lawless reputation is yet more evidence that it should be permanently reunited with the Spanish mainland. In a community with only 30,000 inhabitants, nearly everyone on the Rock knows the men who work for the drug barons. Their tinted-window cars thud rap music out of rattling speakers as they coast up and down the colony's tacky high street stuck in second gear. Yet they remain relatively untouched by authorities.

The irony behind the influx of British villains into Gibraltar is that many of them are drawn to the Rock from their whitewashed villas on the Costa del Sol by the very Britishness of the place. Back in 2000, Spanish Prime Minister José Maria Aznar handed Tony Blair a file on alleged criminal activity on the Rock, which claimed that criminals, including at least six UK firms, in Gibraltar had begun turning their hand to murder and kidnappings connected to their big-money criminal enterprises.

Down at the Rock's Queensway Quay Marina, favourable mooring rates and luxurious amenities have even persuaded some of the Costa del Sol's flashier villains to keep their yachts there when they are not out sailing. Every now and again Gibraltar's government is reminded by the big chiefs in Whitehall that they should crack down on the drug barons. Then orders are issued to seize a few of the smugglers' favourite boats, the rigid inflatables. But, as happened a few years back, the owners of these crafts (the drug barons never have legally proven ownership) erupt, battle the police and cause a bit of mayhem.

The result? A discreet pause and then the boats are given back and business carries on as usual. The Rock's authorities even introduced a law banning any further importation of rigid inflatables. Owners of such boats were ordered to show evidence that they were used for bona fide purposes. 'Now everyone who owns an inflatable has paperwork proving that he does boat trips for tourists,' says one Gibraltar regular. 'The law was a waste of time but at least it shut Whitehall up.'

But the other important reason why so many British criminals use Gibraltar as a base for their dodgy enterprises is because the Rock is awash with funny money – forged currency and black cash from the proceeds of crime. Of the £3.5 billion floating around Gibraltar, more than half of it is reckoned to be the proceeds of illicit business dealings, smuggling and drug trafficking.

Back in the mid-1990s, the US Drugs Enforcement Agency and the British government set up Operation

Dinero. Authorities created a fake offshore bank in the British dependency of Anguilla and the cash soon started rolling in – from Gibraltar, no less. Offshore investors in the Rock had included such luminaries as pension-sapping newspaper baron Robert Maxwell and fraudster Peter Clowes of Barlow Clowes – a big player on the Rock – who was convicted of diddling investors out of £150 million. Recently, Spanish authorities were horrified when they established links between the Basque separatist group ETA and money-laundering operations based in Gibraltar. They have no doubt that the British-run colony is inadvertently helping fund ETA bombings and killings in Spain.

One of the few Gibraltar-based villains to be actually nicked in recent years was Pasquale Locatelli, who used shipping companies based on the Rock to launder the proceeds of crime. Locatelli had connections with Rome mafia boss Roberto Severa as well as Sicilian mafia moneyman Pippo Calo. Even Roberto Calvi, 'God's Banker', who was found hanging under Blackfriars Bridge after his bank slid into fraudulent bankruptcy in 1982, was linked to Locatelli and other Gibraltar-based individuals.

And then there is the latest money-obsessed boom to hit the Rock: gambling. While there is no suggestion that the spate of new betting enterprises are connected to criminals, gambling has made Gibraltar an even more attractive proposition to any Costa del Sol-based villain who fancies a flutter. In the past couple of years, Victor Chandler, Ladbrokes, Coral and Stan James have all set up betting operations from the Rock. They all insist that Gibraltar is ideal for them because of its favourable tax breaks, the English-speaking workforce and decent weather. 'Gibraltar is booming financially and a lot of it has to be down to the drug barons, money launderers and corrupt businesses,' says one former Gibraltar resident, Chris Coombes. 'If the UK tries to clean it up then it will rapidly slide into complete and utter financial collapse and that's when the Spanish will move in and make their strongest claim yet to rescue the colony.'

In other words, the criminals are good news for Gibraltar. It's a sad irony.

CHAPTER SIXTEEN

THE ONE THAT DIDN'T GET AWAY

Kenneth Noye hoped to evade
justice in Spain

THE ONE THAT DIDN'T GET AWAY

In the Costa del Sol underworld, certain names resonate for the sheer, stunning audacity of their crimes. They are admired by new and old gangsters, they have the police in their pockets and they live on the very edge. Meet Kenny Noye.

Noye was – and still is – one of the most powerful and richest criminals in Britain. A genius of the underworld, handling the proceeds of huge drug deals and legendary robberies have helped make him tens of millions of pounds. He had a string of women scattered around the globe and he enjoyed a five-star lifestyle. He is also another member of that exclusive gentlemen gangsters' club, the Brinks Mat team. It is a legendary job that links so many of the criminals who have settled on the Costa del Sol. Noye's emergence as a major player is an integral part of recent criminal history – but how did he end up in Spain?

Kenneth John Noye was born in Bexleyheath, Kent, on 24 May 1947. His father Jim was a telecommunications expert at the GPO; his mum Edith was a strong, plain-speaking lady who took her young son under her wing from an early age. She worked three nights a week as manageress of the nearby Crayford dog track. Schoolboy Noye was a charming, troublesome kid. These days they'd call him hyperactive. 'He got away with a lot because he was very cheeky,' his cousin Michael Noye told me a few years back. 'But he couldn't keep out of trouble for a minute. A right handful.' Young Noye was already boasting about what he'd do when he grew up. 'Earn lots of money,' he pledged to anyone who would listen.

Teenage Noye kicked off his criminal career at Bexleyheath secondary modern when he leaned on other school kids for protection money. A brief spell at printing college followed, but that soon gave way to stealing cars and scooters and selling them on to other villains in south-east London and Kent. Then Noye started a lorry haulage business and was soon making a fortune handling stolen property.

Noye married his teenage sweetheart Brenda and soon had two sons, Brett and Kevin. They moved to the peace and quiet of a village called West Kingsdown; situated in the Kent countryside, it was still within shotgun range of his old south-east London haunts. That's when Noye began fronting the cash for some daring robberies. One former associate explained, 'Noye was soon handling half a dozen jobs at a time. The money was rolling in.' The beauty of Noye's criminal career was that he rarely got his own hands dirty. He'd simply put up the finance for a job and then leave it up to his team.

By the time Noye had turned 30, he was driving a Rolls Royce and juggling a handful of fancy women; he even had time to become a Mason in a cheeky bid to get closer to the other members who included policemen, judges and politicians. As one Kent policeman later explained, 'Noye cynically manoeuvred himself into the Masons as if it was the right pub for him to be seen at.'

On 10 October 1981, Noye appeared in Canterbury Crown Court for charges including importation of a firearm, evasion of VAT, providing a counterfeit document after his arrest and breaking the conditions of an earlier suspended sentence. He was very lucky to get a suspended prison sentence plus a £2,500 fine. Many believe to this day that Noye's 'friends' in the Kent constabulary helped him avoid a spell inside.

Noye was then put under regular police surveillance. A crime intelligence report at the time stated that Noye was running a stolen motor-vehicle-parts ring, which also involved exporting lorry equipment to Syria. He was even rumoured to have supplied some of the heavy-lifting vehicles used to construct the Thames Barrier. Noye had a finger in a hell of lot of pies.

Using the alias of Kenneth James, he also kept a luxury flat in Broomfield Road, Bexleyheath, where neighbours spotted him in the company of numerous

men and women. Police soon linked Noye to more than
a dozen companies, and his list of 'associates' read like
a who's who of the south-east London and Kent
underworld. Besides his Rolls Royce, Noye drove a Jeep
and various Fords, which he had bought directly from
Fords in Dagenham through a contact. Noye sold them
on later for a fat profit.

One of Noye's former employees at his lorry yard in
West Kingsdown told the police he was terrified of the
criminal and stated that he had 'suffered violence at the
hands of Noye in the past'. Even back in the early-1980s,
the police reckoned Kenny was dabbling in the drugs
trade. On one occasion they watched him pass over
£10,000 in cash to an unnamed man in the Black Swan
pub on Mile End Road in the East End. They believed it
was drug money. The police report at the time stated,
'Noye allegedly puts up the money for organised crime,
he is an associate of prominent London criminals. Noye
travels to and from America and the Continent to
allegedly change money.'

Noye also provided hundreds of thousands of stolen
bricks for the construction of a housing estate called The
Hollies in Gravesend, Kent. And the secret police report
even named an MP with whom Noye 'had a business
association'. Noye and a few other local criminals even
occasionally collected 'reward money' for pointing the
police in the right direction, which enabled him to keep
all his own illegal activities going unhindered.

But it was the Brinks Mat robbery that really put
Kenny Noye on the map and gave him respect

throughout the London underworld. He handled much of the £27 million worth of gold bullion stolen from a warehouse near Heathrow Airport in November 1983. Later, Noye stabbed to death an undercover policeman carrying out a surveillance operation in Noye's garden. Noye was acquitted of murdering the officer but got 14 years for VAT fraud in connection with the stolen gold.

In 1987, during a spell inside the relatively easygoing HMP Swaleside on Noye's manor of Kent, he met a drugs peddler with a deadly reputation called Pat Tate who told him all about a new designer drug called ecstasy, which was just starting to take off in Britain. Tate convinced Noye to invest £30,000 in one of his ecstasy deals. Many villains reckon that it was the start of millions of pounds of Brinks Mat cash that helped flood Britain with ecstasy in the late-1980s and early-1990s. (Tate, his partner Tony Tucker and another drug dealer called Craig Rolfe were later shot to death at point-blank range as they sat in their Range Rover in an Essex field.) Legend has it that Noye made £200,000 back from that original £30,000 investment. From inside prison, he invested vast sums of his considerable fortune – estimated in the late 1980s at £10 million – in the drugs explosion.

In May 1996 Noye, released from prison just 18 months earlier, made the biggest mistake of his life when he knifed to death motorist Stephen Cameron in a road-rage attack on the M25, just a few miles from his Kent home. Within hours of fleeing the scene, Noye was in a chopper rising above the countryside just outside

Bristol to begin a two-and-a-half-year spell on the run from the police. Back on the ground, Noye's brand-new Land Rover Discovery containing the knife he'd used to kill Stephen Cameron was being driven in a bizarre three-car convoy to Dartford, Kent, where it was scrapped by being crushed into a compressed box of jagged steel.

In 1997, Noye sneaked into southern Spain and turned up in an isolated village north-west of Marbella. He continued popping back and forth to south-east London for important meetings. He even financed a daring plot to spring a drug baron from inside HMP Whitemoor in Cambridgeshire. It involved smuggling in quantities of Semtex explosive, blasting a hole in the jail wall and then flying their man to freedom in a chopper. But the escape plan was foiled just days before it was due to go ahead.

Meanwhile, his costs for staying on the run at his Spanish hideaway were rocketing. He was shelling out £30,000 a month to keep one step ahead of the police. 'He was greasing palms, paying for birds, his missus, you name it. And he was having to only deal in cash otherwise the cozzers might get wind of his movements,' explained one of his old Costa del Sol mates who saw him occasionally while he was on the run.

But Noye's life on the run in the Costa del Sol didn't stop him from earning tens of millions of pounds in drug deals from his Spanish hideaway. He even boasted that he was still paying off crooked cops back in the UK. Noye was so heavily involved in cannabis smuggling that he visited Yardies in Jamaica while he was on the run. He was monitored by British police in Gibraltar with a local drug baron, but no one recognised him. Noye travelled in and out of Gibraltar on a false UK passport without even having to show his photo ID and was photographed by the Spanish police with a local girlfriend called Mina because she was under surveillance. But again, no one recognised him.

On the Spanish mainland, Noye bought a luxury yacht for £200,000 and chartered it out to drugs smugglers. And he so terrified the owner of the house he had bought in the tiny village of Atlanterra, 75 miles north-west of Marbella, that the man went into hiding in Germany after accepting Noye's offer of cash, no questions asked.

He also pulled a knife on a middle-aged neighbour in Atlanterra when the man climbed over his gate to talk to his gardener. Frequently he secretly smuggled his father, wife Brenda and other relatives and mates to his home in Spain even though the police back in Kent were supposed to be shadowing their every move. And Noye wasn't even spotted when 20 Spanish policemen patrolled the next-door house because one of Spain's most senior politicians spent the summer at the property. Throughout his stay in Spain, Noye flew various mistresses out to Portugal then smuggled them across the border and rented them isolated houses at least ten miles from his own home.

In mid-June 1998, police back in Kent had a lucky break when they got a call from a long-time informant who gave them the mobile phone number of another villain who was in regular contact with Noye. When the grass demanded a £100,000 tip-off fee if it led detectives to Noye, the police started to take him very seriously.

Kent police immediately requested assistance from MI5, who sanctioned round-the-clock surveillance of the target's phone from their headquarters overlooking Vauxhall Bridge in London. MI5, Britain's domestic security service, has some sophisticated surveillance equipment and had been helping the police across the country with their enquiries since the mid-1990s. By the end of August 1998, Noye had been traced to his house in Atlanterra. Days later, he was arrested in a nearby restaurant by Spanish and Kent police and taken to jail in nearby Cadiz. His beautiful brunette girlfriend disappeared into thin air as the cops swooped.

Noye's team of highly paid Spanish lawyers reckoned he stood a good chance of avoiding extradition back to the UK. In the spring of 1999, Madrid judges threw out all of Noye's appeals and, after a couple of last-ditch appeals by his briefs had failed, Noye was handcuffed and ordered out of his cell at Madrid's Valdemoro jail. He was bundled into an anonymous white van escorted by two plain saloons out towards the city suburbs. Less than 30 minutes later, Noye was handed over to three Kent policemen at Madrid Airport and secretly flown to London's Gatwick Airport.

Back in England, the London underworld was buzzing with rumours about who'd grassed up Kenny Noye. Stories were circulating that the informant had qualified for £100,000 reward money; but would he live long enough to enjoy it? As one criminal source at the time said, 'I can tell you there will be an even bigger price on that bastard's head for turning in Kenny Noye.'

Noye even let it be known that he was so confident he'd be acquitted of the murder of Stephen Cameron that he'd authorised his sidekick in Spain, James Stewart, to get his house ready for his return. He even bunged thousands of pounds to his builder back in Spain from his prison cell. 'He was that confident he'd get off. His cronies were spreading the gospel according to Noye around the entire prison. It's a game that Noye is very good at,' explained another inmate.

When Noye walked into the number two court of the Old Bailey on Thursday, 30 March 2000, he was grey haired and dressed in a grey cardigan. He sat hunched almost like an old man in the dock between three prison officers. His eyes panned the jury of eight women and four men from the moment he was led in by three prison screws. Noye claimed he was simply defending himself when he pulled a knife out from under the front seat of his car and knifed Cameron to death on the M25 roundabout. But the jury didn't believe him and found him guilty of murder by a verdict of 11–1.

In the hours following the verdict, it emerged that Noye's defence, estimated to have cost between £500,000 and £1million, had been funded by the taxpayer. He'd been granted legal aid because on paper he was not worth a penny.

Noye still currently owns a share in a hotel in Spain, a

timeshare holiday complex in Northern Cyprus and two penthouse apartments in a nearby town in Cyprus. His wife lives in a detached bungalow in Looe, Cornwall. His parents live in a recently built detached five-bedroom house on his old manor of West Kingsdown, Kent. Then there is the semi in Bexleyheath, which he has in the past used to 'entertain' his women friends.

Noye, the master manipulator, remains locked up in top-security HMP Whitemoor plotting his next move. Underworld sources initially believed Noye would name some top faces to the police in exchange for a reduced sentence. But then the key witness against Noye during the Cameron murder trial was gunned down by a hitman outside a shopping centre in Kent in the late summer of 2000. The murdered witness's wife told a newspaper that she did not believe her husband had told the truth during Noye's Old Bailey trial. Shortly afterwards, Noye's legal team announced that they were putting together a serious appeal against his murder conviction. His lawyers were eventually granted a full appeal against his conviction and he is currently pursuing the case through the European Court of Human Rights. His lawyers have already had his minimum sentence reduced to 16 years, and the building work at his home in Spain has been completed at a cost of many tens of thousands of pounds because Noye believes he will one day be released. He plans to spend his remaining years on his beloved Costa del Crime.

CHAPTER SEVENTEEN
UNDERCOVER COP

Melting into anonymity – 'Micky'
keeps it undercover

UNDERCOVER COP

The Costa del Crime is, as you've no doubt already worked out, a hotbed of lawbreakers and vice. For the past 20 years, the Spanish police have allowed teams of British detectives to operate in the area. In January 2004, Detective Sergeant Paul Finnigan, 41, was knifed outside a restaurant in Fuengirola after he had been transferred by Northamptonshire police to the National Crime Squad to investigate a drugs ring based in the area.

Spanish police say they are happy to allow the British cops to operate on their territory because it can be a useful deterrent to these UK criminals. As one Spanish detective told me recently, 'We know very little about these people when they show up from Britain, so we need the British police to help us arrest them. Also, many of their criminal enterprises are linked between

Spain and the UK, so offences have been committed in both countries.'

Micky from east London is a classic example of the type of hardened police detective who works on the Costa del Crime. He had one major world player in the cocaine business under observation for many months. Micky explains, 'It's a much riskier business being out here watching villains because there's none of the backup we get back home. If any of these characters suss out they're being watched, they can become very dangerous. Two of my colleagues were beaten to a pulp by one drug baron's henchmen when he found out we were spying on him. Back in the UK he would never have dared attack the police in that way, but out here anything goes.'

Micky is hardly what you might call a traditional-looking Scotland Yard copper. He's got shoulder-length hair, a muscular, stocky body and a Santa Claus-style beard that makes him look a lot older than his 39 years. 'My job was to infiltrate a gang of drugs smugglers who were importing cocaine from South America and paying runners to drive the drugs through Europe back to Britain. It was a very sophisticated operation, very slick and well organised. The guy who was running it was a hardened, old-school gangster and I had to work my way in.'

Micky – who's done a spot of bare-knuckle fighting in his time – managed to get himself work as an enforcer, or debt collector, for the gang. 'Luckily, I had the contacts back in the East End who vouched for me so I was able to get into the gang quite easily.' Proving what they were up to was a different kettle of fish. 'This lot were mega-careful,' recalls Micky. 'Even their drug runners were followed by other members of the gang to make sure they weren't police grasses. No one was trusted apart from the men right at the very top. I was taken on two or three debt-collecting operations and had to actually threaten a couple of fellows who hadn't paid their drug debts, but this was chicken-feed for us because it didn't prove anything against the Mr Big who was running the operation. I had to be patient and wait for the right type of evidence to materialise which we could then use in a court of law.'

For the next six months, Micky ate, slept and drank with the gang and was never once able to call his wife and three kids back in the East End. 'That was fucking hard on me and my family, but we simply couldn't afford to risk blowing my cover. These fellas were so careful, I wouldn't have been surprised if they were monitoring my mobile phone calls. Some nights I'd collapse exhausted into the bed at my tiny apartment and wonder what the fuck I was doing there. All I wanted was to be at home with my wife and kids back in the normal world.'

Micky kept going for a very good reason. 'A nephew of mine died from a heroin overdose,' he reveals, 'and it was so fucking sad to see what that did to his family. These evil bastards who sell drugs have no idea about the misery they're causing to normal, law-abiding families. Every time I got close to quitting that job in

Spain, I thought of my nephew and realised I had to keep going.'

Careful about communicating with his police bosses back in London, Micky only used internet cafés to contact them. 'And then I used a pseudonym in case anyone back in London grassed me up to the villains I was working for in Spain. In this game, you can't trust anyone, not even the detectives you work with day in, day out.'

Eventually Micky found himself completely accepted into the gang, which was based in Torremolinos, and was told by his new boss that he was required to travel to South America to provide protection for the gang while they met cocaine barons in Cali, Colombia. 'It was the last thing I wanted,' says Micky, 'because there was no way I could travel to another country with them as I couldn't risk a problem with a false passport. But without going on such operations with them I couldn't gather enough direct evidence to ensure they would all go down for a very long time.'

Micky had no choice but to pretend he was seriously ill and cry off the Colombia trip. 'They were right pissed off with me and started looking at me like I wasn't to be trusted. That's a bad moment in any undercover copper's life. It means people start asking questions and there's a risk they might find out the truth.' Within days, Micky's bosses pulled him out of Spain. 'I was willing to carry on, but they said it was too big a risk. I was very disappointed because I genuinely wanted to nick this lot, big time. They were a bunch of evil bastards who didn't give a flying fuck about anyone. What bugs me now is that no one has since managed to infiltrate that gang as successfully as I did, which means they're still thriving. This can be one hell of frustrating job at times. I just hope we get them one day.'

Micky quit the police in late 2003 and got himself a job as a security consultant. He explains, 'I truly loved the job but, after what happened in Spain, everything seemed a bit mundane. I found it really difficult back in London dealing with domestic crimes and burglaries after what I'd been through. In the end I knew I had to make a fresh start away from the force. Some of my best mates are still in the job but it's not for me any more. Maybe if I'd never gone to Spain in the first place then I'd still be a happy detective aiming for thirty years' service and a nice fat pension, but that's just not the way it turned out.'

CHAPTER EIGHTEEN
RUBIO CHRIS

Chris Lees in Bristol – the Costa
can wait

RUBIO CHRIS

He's called Rubio because of the blond hair and fair skin, which used to turn red in the searing Costa del Crime sunshine. The word means blond in Spanish. But Oldham-born Chris Lees is anything but a typical Brit in Spain. This 42-year-old entrepreneur has had his finger in a lot of pies, and he nearly paid for it with his life.

Chris first arrived in Fuengirola back in the mid-1980s. In those days, he explains, he was 'nothing more than a daft kid ready to try his hand at anything. I was after an adventure, but I didn't have a brass farthing to my name, so I started getting involved in some right dodgy capers.' Chris soon found himself working as a tobacco smuggler, illegally importing Spain's dirt-cheap cigarettes into the UK. 'Back then it was a great way to earn a decent wedge,' says Chris. 'It wasn't like drugs smuggling and most Customs guys turned a blind eye because they had more important things to worry about.'

As a tobacco smuggler, Chris found himself mixing with 'some right dodgy geezers' and he also worked from some bizarre locations. 'There was one supermarket in Fuengirola where all the big Brit villains hung out in the canteen in the daytime,' says Chris. 'You could buy anything from an AK-47 rifle to a dodgy passport in that place. There was always some scumbag sitting supping a beer, ready to help.' Being a tobacco smuggler brought Chris into contact with some major criminal faces and on a couple of occasions he upset a few of them.

'I tend to be pretty straightforward, and a lot of them didn't like that one bit. In the end I got forced out of the smuggling game and life became much more of a struggle.'

Chris quit Spain in the early-1990s and returned to the UK, but the lure of sunshine, easy money and easy women proved too strong. In 1998 he slipped back to Spain and his old haunts in Fuengirola. 'That's when my problems really kicked off. I should have stayed back in Britain, but I was addicted to that Spanish lifestyle. It seemed so much better than cold, bitter, grey England.'

Chris set up a combined restaurant and disco in Fuengirola; it was a roaring success. Word soon got around that he was making a lot of money and some of the local unsavoury characters decided they wanted a share of his profits. 'A bunch of British crims turned up one night asking questions about me and saying that they'd heard there was a group of fellas going around

Fuengirola, wrecking clubs. What they really meant was that they were going to trash my place unless I bunged them some protection money. Well, I wasn't going to stand for that. So I told them all to fuck off, which didn't go down too well. Next thing I know, the Spanish police are threatening to withdraw my licence.' It was then that Chris Lees found out what a lonely place the Costa del Crime can be if you're not in with the right people.

'A few days later, I'm nicked by the police on suspicion of being involved in some kind of drugs ring. It was outrageous. The cops claimed that I had knowingly rented my house out to a bunch of cocaine smugglers and that I was part of their gang. The whole thing was a fit-up, and I immediately knew those Brit crims had grassed me up because I wouldn't pay them protection money.'

Chris was flung into a notorious men's prison north of Malaga, where he was locked up for almost a year before the police released him without charge. 'It was a bad time. I kept insisting I was innocent, but so do most people in prison so no one was interested in listening to me. At one stage I thought I'd be sentenced to ten years when the detectives interrogated me and I refused to answer their questions.' Chris was released in the summer of 2002 with no warning.

'They just opened my cell one morning and said I was free to go. No apology, nothing.' Chris was, by his own account, 'a changed man. I didn't trust anyone any more. I had a shorter temper and I was, quite frankly, very resentful at my treatment by the police and prison staff. The jail was a shithole and I found myself sharing cells with some right nutters. It was something I hope never happens to me again.'

Back in the real world, Chris soon discovered that most of his old mates in Fuengirola didn't want to know him any more. 'They all thought I'd grassed someone up in order to get released. People would abuse me in the street and I couldn't walk into a bar without it going silent. It was a horrible feeling and I realised I had to get away and start afresh somewhere else.'

So Chris quit Spain and moved to Bristol where he had a few old friends. He set up a limousine-rental company, which is now highly successful, and has even managed to be elected a local councillor. 'Prison taught me never to waste a moment. Since arriving back here I've started over and it's been fantastic. I'll never go back to live in Spain again, and whenever I talk to any friends over there they always sound either very bored or very broke – or both! The Costa del Sol rots people's brains, if you know what I mean. It's an evil place filled with nasty opportunists who'd quite happily stitch up their grannies given the chance. I'm better off out of there now.'

CHAPTER NINEEEN
THE PIMPERNEL

They may well be seeking him
here and there, but Mickey Green
is definitely the one in the middle

THE PIMPERNEL

Costa del Crime resident Mickey Green, described by Eire's Criminal Assets Bureau as one of the world's biggest cocaine traffickers, has become so adept at escaping justice since his days as a notorious London armed robber 30 years ago that he has been nicknamed the Pimpernel by authorities. These days he spends much of his time in Spain, having been released after legal argument. Green is the classic Mr Big, with alleged links to the Mafia and Colombian drug cartels.

His grand-looking hacienda just east of Marbella is worth more than £2 million, and he even has a friend to live in one of the nearby houses to keep an eye on the property whenever he is on his travels. As one of his Costa del Crime mates says, 'Mickey's from the old school. He's done well for himself and kept on his toes for much of the past twenty-five years. Good luck to him!'

Now 62 years old, Green has over the years been shadowed by UK, Dutch and French authorities, who suspect him of major criminal activities. British Customs agents have pursued Green for years. One told me, 'We'll get Mickey one day. It's just a matter of time. He thinks he's cleverer than us, but one day he'll make a mistake.'

Michael John Paul Green was born in 1942 in Wembley to a family originally from Ireland, and is described by many who know him as a good old-fashioned London villain. He is also said to be your original medallion man with a taste for birds and booze. He first made his criminal reputation back in 1972 when a notorious London supergrass called Bertie Smalls named him as leader of a gang of robbers known as the Wembley Mob – then the UK's most successful team of armed blaggers. Green was eventually jailed for 18 years for his part in the 1970 robbery of a bank in Ilford that yielded £237,000, although he was suspected of involvement in numerous other crimes.

Green got out on parole after serving seven years of his sentence, and was soon back in the thick of things. He teamed up with old Wembley Mob partner Ronnie Dark, and they developed a lucrative VAT scam on gold krugerrands. They bought the gold coins – which didn't carry VAT – then melted them down into ingots – which did – and sold them back to the bullion house, collecting a hefty wedge of VAT in the process. It is reckoned that Mickey and his pals made £6 million in under a year. 'It was a brilliant scam,' says one of his friends in Spain who has known Green for many years. 'Mickey's always had an eye for the main chance. He couldn't resist the gold scam and it made him a fortune.'

When the police and Customs agents moved in on the gang in London in the early-1980s, Green hotfooted it to the Costa del Crime. One of his closest mates in the sunshine was Frank Maple. They were both perfectly at ease among the thousands of recent ex-pats colonising the Costa del Sol. Maple had fled to Spain after being named as the brains behind the infamous Bank of America robbery in Mayfair in 1975. He also spent three years in an Austrian jail for a £100,000 hotel robbery. Others noticed that Green and Maple seemed to have limitless spending power.

Some have described the Costa del Crime at this time as being like the Wild West. One old-timer explained, 'The heaviest, hardest faces were living here then because there was still no proper extradition treaty between Spain and the UK.' Kidnaps, robberies and killings were being ordered by some of the UK's most notorious criminals who were based in Spain at the time. No one knows if Green was ever involved in such activities, but he was certainly not shy about throwing his cash around. Back then he was living in a luxury penthouse in the La Nogalera building in Torremolinos, driving a white Rolls Royce and a red Porsche. He also had his own yacht and had become a regular at many of Marbella's most exclusive restaurants and clubs.

During the 1980s, Green started building up a vast drug empire, using Spain as his centre of operations to run narcotics into Europe from North Africa. In 1987 he was arrested by Spanish police after two tons of hashish was seized. Green was given bail and fled to Morocco, leaving behind 11 powerboats and yachts allegedly used to run drugs from North Africa.

Then Green turned up in Paris and Interpol were alerted. French police swooped on his swish Left Bank apartment, where they found gold bullion and cocaine but no Mickey Green. He was later sentenced to 17 years in jail in his absence for possession of drugs and smuggling. Green's next stop was California, where he rented Rod Stewart's mansion under an alias.

A few months later, FBI agents knocked his front door down as he was lounging by the pool and arrested him. Green was put on a flight bound for France and that jail sentence, but got off when the plane made a stopover at Ireland's Shannon Airport. Using his Irish passport, he slipped unnoticed past Customs men and headed for Dublin where he had many contacts. Green then took full advantage of the weak extradition laws between Eire and France at the time and settled in Dublin. He even splashed out on a massive half-million-pound farmhouse just outside the city.

In 1995 Green ran a red light at a busy junction in his Bentley and killed taxi driver Joe White. He was fined and banned from driving, but there was uproar in the local press because he was not given a custodial sentence, despite the death of an innocent man. Under mounting pressure, Eire police made it clear that they were planning to grab Green's assets, including his

but smuggling charges against Green were dropped after we decided that the evidence from his former associate Michael Michael was not strong enough to bring a prosecution back in Britain.'

After Michael's arrest by Customs officers in 1998, he had named Green a Mr Big of the drugs world. At Michael's eventual trial at the Old Bailey in 2001, prosecutor Nicholas Loraine-Smith said that Mickey Green was a major drug baron. He said, 'He was and continues to be involved in importing large amounts of drugs into this country.' It was said after Michael's trial that Green had recruited Michael to head the UK end of his huge cocaine and cannabis smuggling racket, and that they both made millions in the process.

Following his arrest and subsequent court case, Michael had good reason to fear the wrath of Mickey Green. It was said in court that Green had organised the murders of two other criminals. First to die was hardman Gilbert Wynter, who disappeared from his north-London home in 1998. His body was rumoured to be in a car crusher or in the foundations of the Millennium Dome. Then a notorious finance chief for a London criminal family was shot dead outside his home. Michael told Customs investigators that they were both killed after double-crossing Green in a half-million-pound cannabis deal.

In the same Old Bailey court case, one of Michael's cash couriers, a woman called Janice Marlborough, said in court that Green was 'head of the tree'. Even today, Green is described in Interpol intelligence reports as a highly dangerous criminal mastermind. Police sources say that Green has surrounded himself with an army of bodyguards and heavies. As one Scotland Yard detective explained, 'If you were ducking and diving for more than forty years as one of the heaviest gangsters in the world, you'd be more than likely to have stepped on a few toes, and Mickey Green is no exception to that rule. If we don't get him, no doubt someone else will.'

These days Green spends much of his time on the Costa del Crime, although sources in Spain say that he is planning to spend increasing amounts of time in Costa Rica where he owns another luxury home. It is also rumoured that he is planning a property purchase in Thailand. As one of those involved in his Barcelona arrest says, 'Mickey's a survivor, but you can be sure he's watching his back very carefully.'

CHAPTER TWENTY
EL GUMSHOE

'Pete' the private eye operates
out of Marbella

EL GUMSHOE

There's a lot of business out there for a good private eye on the Costa del Crime. 'Pete' hails from Cheshire originally, but we cannot use his real name here because only Spanish nationals are allowed to get licences to work as private investigators.

'It's bloody daft, really,' says Pete. 'I can't be legal here, so I have to run everything out of a mailbox address back in the UK so that I'm not breaking any laws in Spain.' Pete is a former police detective who fell in love with Spain when he spent two weeks on the coast investigating a gang of Merseyside-based drugs smugglers. 'Back then I was a bit of a green young copper and some of the things I stumbled upon in Spain came as quite a culture shock. But I loved the Spanish attitude towards enjoying life to the full. They're much more relaxed than the British and I found that very appealing.'

Four years ago, bachelor Pete quit the police and headed down to the Costa del Crime. 'I knew a few people on both sides of the law down here, and they kept saying there was plenty of work for a good private eye because a lot of the Brits don't trust the Spanish investigators. This is very unfair on the Spaniards, but it's the way it is with many of the Brits here, and I could see where the opportunities would come from.'

Pete discreetly placed adverts in local English-speaking publications along the coast, emphasising that he was based in Britain but able to carry out inquiries all along the southern Spanish coast. 'That way I knew that the Spanish couldn't try and shut me down because I didn't have a licence to operate here,' he explained. 'I was soon flooded with work. Much of it is for divorce cases because so many men fall for the sex and drugs lifestyle out here that their marriages soon go belly-up.'

Pete is based in a rented apartment just behind Marbella old town. It's a modest place, but it serves the purpose. 'I have to keep a low profile, and it has to look as if I am only a visitor because of the licence problems. But I've never been one for possessions and owning property. It suits me down to the ground.'

Recently, Pete was hired by a 'very wealthy' woman to spy on the husband she suspected of having an affair. 'This woman just called me up out of the blue after seeing one of my adverts. She said she'd pay a very generous daily rate if I would just shadow her old man for a few weeks to see what he was up to.

'I thought it was a bit odd when she insisted on

meeting me in the car park of a McDonald's in San Pedro before starting the case. When I asked her why, she said she was scared that her husband might find out what she was up to. Well, as soon as I met her, I was convinced she had to be married to a gangster. She turned up in a new Mercedes sports car, dripping in gold, heavily tanned with a peroxide rinse, and she wasn't able to tell me specifically what her husband did for a job. She just said in a very strong east London accent that her old man was a property speculator. I didn't believe a word of it.

'I had a bit of a bad feeling about it, and started to hesitate about taking the job. Then she offered me a thousand euros a day so I went for it. Money speaks louder than words, and I've been around for long enough to know how to follow someone without them knowing it, so I reckoned the risk was minimal. The only thing that really bothered me was that all this money she was paying me probably came from drugs, but it wasn't really my problem.'

For the following few weeks, Pete shadowed his target using all his police experience. 'Instead of going behind his car, I went in front. It's very effective because no one studies the vehicles ahead of them. I soon discovered that the wife was perfectly right to be suspicious of her husband. This guy didn't just have a mistress, he had an insatiable appetite for sex. He was using some of the Costa del Sol's most notorious brothels virtually every day and he had three regular girls set up in separate apartments along the coast. The guy was addicted to screwing.'

But when Pete reported back to the man's wife what he'd seen, there was an awkward response. 'She went all quiet after I sat her down and told her. Instead of bursting into tears, she just kept nodding her head slowly and saying, "Right." I then asked her what she was going to do with the information I had given her, and she snapped back at me that it was none of my business. I started to get a bit worried then, because in my game the last thing you want is a bitter wife exposing your identity to a cheating husband, especially if he is a major criminal. I tried to explain nicely to her that she could not reveal my identity to anyone, let alone her hubby. But she then coolly turned to me and said, "I'm afraid he already knows all about you."

'"What?" I said to her.

'"He was having me watched by one of his mates and they saw us in the car park when we first met," she told me. "He thought you and I were having a fling, so I had to come clean and tell him the truth."

'Well, my heart sank when I heard her. It was a disaster. The husband might come after me, especially if he got paranoid that I'd seen any of his criminal activities, which I hadn't. I then asked her if she had told her hubby precisely what I'd seen him get up to. She even let it drop that he was very angry I'd been spying on him.

'"I had to tell him," she told me. "Now he's promised to drop all the women in the flats and not go to brothels any more." I didn't have the heart to tell her that he'd never change his ways because men just don't do that on the whole, especially big-time villains. Now my main priority was to ease out of this job without being physically harmed by this woman's husband.'

Pete then decided, in his words, 'to enter the lion's den. I reckoned it was safer to meet this character than try and run away from him. It was a gamble, but it had to be done so I phoned him up and arranged to meet him in a very public place so that he couldn't let his heavies loose on me.' It turned out to be a clever move. 'He was very upset at first and called me a piece of scum – which seemed a bit rich coming from him. But then he said he was impressed I'd had the courage to meet him and we actually got on quite well. He even told me his missus had hired two other Spanish private investigators before me who had both fleeced her of money and done nothing. He seemed to find that quite funny. And when I asked him how he'd found out she had hired those two earlier investigators, he replied, "Silly bitch paid those two muppets on her credit card. I couldn't miss it."

'I also recognised that this villain had so many contacts along the coast that could become an invaluable source for me. We've stayed in touch ever since.'

On another occasion late in 2003, Pete was hired by the private secretary of a mega-wealthy prince from a foreign royal family living in Marbella, who suspected one of his most senior advisors of dealing in massive quantities of cocaine bought from a Russian drug gang. 'They thought this bloke was dealing drugs big time, and were very worried that if he was arrested by the police it would embarrass this royal family,' remembered Pete. 'Basically they wanted me to get the evidence so they could confront him and then quietly fire him before a scandal erupted.'

Pete spent two months shadowing the prince's advisor, mainly around the wealthy resort of Puerto Banus. 'The strange thing was that, for the first six weeks, he didn't go near anyone who even vaguely looked like a drug supplier, let alone a Russian,' says Pete. 'I was about to recommend to the client that we end the surveillance operation when my man walked into a bar in Puerto Banus that was notorious for its criminal clientele. I was standing right by him when he met with a young-looking eastern-European type of man. He had quite gay mannerisms, and even though my target was married with two children I wondered if they were secret lovers.

'Then I saw this other man handing my target a sachet of something when they shook hands goodbye. I followed my target outside to where he'd parked his car in a side street. The moment he got in that vehicle, I watched him open up the sachet and take a massive snort of what was obviously cocaine. He did exactly the same thing the following three nights and it became clear that, rather than being a drug dealer, this man was using cocaine for his own personal consumption. That's a different matter altogether, and I told my client that instead of firing this man they should try and persuade him to get help in beating his addiction; I later heard that he got kicked out of his job, which seems a pity – but it's not something I'll lose any sleep over.'

Pete reckons he earns upwards of €100,000 a year working as a private eye on the Costa del Crime, and he loves the lifestyle. 'I know how you can get sucked into the drugs and sex stuff out here because I've seen it with my own eyes. I lead a quiet, simple life when I'm not working. I have a very nice Spanish girlfriend, and love nothing more than a glass of Rioja and some tapas when I'm off duty. I leave all the other stuff to the sort of characters who end up coming to me for help.'

But Pete is realistic about his future. 'It's getting more and more dangerous out here, with gangsters flooding the place from all over the world. That makes it more difficult for straight investigators like me to operate. I think a time will come when I'll have to think about another career change, but for the moment I'm very happy with my life.'

CHAPTER TWENTY-ONE
WISE MAN TONY

With clever money-making
scheme, Tony's even wiser than
he looks

WISE MAN TONY

Tony Wiseman's calling card is evidence that he's locked into one of the smartest businesses on the Costa del Crime. Tony, who hails from the UK seaside resort of Brighton, Sussex, is one of a growing breed of unofficial bookies who are cleaning up among the Brits in southern Spain. 'It's fantastic out here. Loads of rich punters, lots of sunshine and nobody breathing down your neck. Who could ask for more?' says Tony, 49, who has made and lost many fortunes over the years.

Tony's patch is three bars close to the waterfront in the Los Boliches area of Fuengirola, a district lived in by more Brits than Spaniards these days. His most important tool is the mobile phone and he – and others like him – are taking full advantage of the fact that bookmakers' shops don't exist in Spain. 'There's an insatiable demand for bookies out here,' says Tony, who lives in a swish penthouse apartment overlooking the beach strip between Benalmadena and Fuengirola with his fiancée Sally. 'When I first came over last year, I really cleaned up. Obviously, as time goes by, more and more fellas will start setting themselves up as bookies and the opportunities for someone like me will begin to fade, but for the moment things are very, very good.'

During a good month, Tony can earn more than €20,000 by taking bets from his mainly British punters. 'There are a lot of bored fellas round here who like a flutter. It's the regulars who are important to me. My idea of a nightmare customer is some bloke on holiday who comes to me with a heavy bet, wins it and then never sets foot back here again. That's a costly experience, I can tell you.'

Tony reckons there are more than two dozen bars along the Costa del Crime where characters like him are taking more than €1,000 a day in bets. 'I wander between the three bars that are on my patch, although many of my customers phone in their bets. I don't like giving credit, but it's better than not taking the bet in the first place.'

If the bets are high, Tony often lays off a portion of the bet with other bookmakers, 'just to water down the risks, if you know what I mean. If another bookie has taken €1,000 on a specific horse, they'll try and lay off €700 of it on someone like me to reduce the risk. I often do the same.'

Tony openly admits pandering to his regular customers, some of whom sound as if they are gambling addicts. 'I've got this one regular who's a doctor. He has lost more than £20,000 with me, and he owed it all because I gave him credit. Well, this bloke was ducking and diving for months. Trying to avoid my calls. Running out of bars when I walked in, all that kind of thing. I was getting right pissed off with him. I even went down to his surgery one day, but his receptionist said he wasn't in. I'm sure she was lying.

'Anyway, it got so bad with this geezer that I had to make it clear that something serious was going to happen to him unless he paid up his debts. He finally came around to my way of thinking – but people like him shouldn't be gambling in the first place. They're completely out of their depth.

'I need regular customers who gamble a certain amount every day. They're like gold-dust. They ring me up on the mobile and ask me what odds I'm offering on certain horses or sports events. I then take that bet. It's entirely my decision what I do with the bet, but you can be sure of one thing – gambling does not pay for the punter. No way.

'A few weeks ago a guy rang me up and said there was

a horse running at Cheltenham the next day and he wanted to put a hefty bet on it, so I said fine. It was a big bet to take because I stood to lose three and a half grand if that horse won. You'd have a job putting a bet on like that in the UK, but I took the bet because that's the way I am – I like to keep my regular customers happy.

'Next morning I woke up in a cold sweat. This bet was really bothering me so I laid it off on another bookie who operates near me. Then I backed that same horse myself to cover my costs and to maybe have the chance of making a few quid myself. Then I found out there were four other horses being heavily betted on in the same race, and I started to get really worried. I thought it might all be some kind of scam. In the end the horse won at 14–1 and I ended up making a packet out of it. But I took the risk in the first place so I reckon I deserved it. That's the name of this game – risk.

'I've been a gambler all my life. Most people lose at the bookies. There's a saying that it's "money lent". As I've said, my regular customers are my vital bread and butter because I know that over a two-year period I'll end up with some, if not all, of their money – and we're talking about many thousands of euros here.'

Tony insists he is not bothered by some of the heavier criminal-type characters who turn to him for a bet. 'Since when did any bookmaker turn away someone's cash because they got it through dodgy activities? There's a load of bored punters out here with plenty of spare cash. Some of them are no doubt genuine retired businessmen, others are villains – but that's none of my business.'

Tony says he is a small-time operator compared with a couple of other bookies who work further down the coast from him. 'There's one bloke here who'll take a twenty-grand bet and he'll lay it off. He's a big risk-taker and sometimes makes a fortune, but he also sometimes loses bucket-loads of cash.'

In recent years, says Tony, more and more of his income has come from what he calls sports betting – especially football, which is getting bigger and bigger – as opposed to horse racing, which is slowly falling away. 'The odds on football are often much more realistic than racing, and it's so incredibly popular at the moment that everyone wants a flutter on a match. There are times on Saturdays and Sundays when I've got the punters literally queuing up in one of my bars to place bets on football matches.'

Tony has this good tip for anyone putting a bet on a football match. 'If you put a bet on a football team scorer and he doesn't end up in the side, you can get that money back from the bookies – although the betting shops don't make much of an effort to let you know it.' Tony reckons more than £20 million in unclaimed bets were kept by major bookies last year. 'The big boys rake in tens of millions. Their profits are in the billions. Little old me isn't doing anyone any harm compared with the big boys.

'Let's face it: Spain will eventually legalise these sort of gambling establishments because there will be so many Brits along the coast that they'll realise they can make a fortune in tax and associated business that will build up once betting shops start opening. But for the moment, they're just going to have to put up with characters like me because the trade is here for everyone, and I'd be a fool if I turned my back on such a brilliant opportunity.'

PART TWO
COSTA DEL SEX

CHAPTER TWENTY-TWO

THE GIGOLO

Steady, ladies, Deano Saunders is
available at reasonable rates

THE GIGOLO

Everyone stopped dead in their tracks as handsome 22-year-old Deano Saunders walked into a busy Marbella bar on the arm of a beautiful blonde older woman. Within seconds, a menacing character with a bulldog neck stepped forward and whispered something in the woman's ear. Deano and his date left the premises immediately. 'I heard later he had a gun and would have used it if we hadn't left – the situation was that heavy,' Deano later recalled. 'He turned out to be her husband's best mate.'

But it's all in a day's work for Deano from Essex, who makes a fortune working as a professional gigolo on the Costa del Crime. Mind you, it's hardly surprising that the well-spoken Psychology graduate has had some close shaves since he started being paid to sleep with women – virtually all British – in the sunshine of Southern Spain.

Deano admits that the incident in the bar did scare him, although his client 'was definitely hoping her hubby would come in. She wanted to make him jealous. I suppose I was lucky it was his best friend rather than the actual husband in that bar. Afterwards, I heard she was married to one of the most notorious drug barons on the entire Costa del Sol. I was lucky to get out of there alive! But at least she paid me £400 for just being on her arm.'

That was just one of many dodgy encounters experienced by Deano. 'Another time I was with a married English woman in her late thirties and her husband insisted on watching us have sex together. Then he suddenly gets up and disappears into another room. I carried on making love to his wife but started to get worried when the husband didn't come back. The woman then kept looking at the door as if she was expecting someone to burst in, so I started to panic because I didn't know what he was up to. Maybe he was going to come back out and attack us. In the end I called out to my bodyguard Chris who was outside, and he immediately started banging on the door. It was a heavy scene: I'd heard of guys who like to watch other men having sex with their wives before beating them to a pulp. I jumped up, grabbed my clothes and, still naked, rushed out of the apartment.'

But there are some unexpected bonuses to the job. Recently, Deano was hired by a middle-of-the-road TV actress. 'I would never reveal who she was,' he explained, 'but she's on the telly all the time in a well-known soap. I couldn't believe it when she turned up. She said she hadn't had sex for months and wanted a really wild night out. First we went out for dinner – she paid, naturally – then it was back to her hotel for a night of passionate lovemaking. She ended up paying me €600 and said I was worth every penny!'

Deano believes the demand for gigolos will increase 'as women get more career minded. There's always been prostitution for men because men always want sex, but now women are wanting their share as their lives become more busy. Also, women seem much lonelier, especially if their marriage isn't going well. A lot of them just want the company, and the sex often takes second place to that.'

Deano even concedes that he has come close to falling in love with a couple of his clients since he arrived on the Costa del Sol in 2002. 'The thing is that these women are often extremely attractive, rich and very amusing company, so it's hardly surprising that I've found many of them genuinely attractive.'

He also reckons that being a gigolo has helped him become much more relaxed in the company of women. 'I'm the furthest from what you would expect of a gigolo. I'm not pushy. I was never the type to chat up girls in clubs, but now I've got more confidence than I've ever had before. I actually believe in myself and my abilities to satisfy a woman.'

Deano first got the idea to work as a gigolo when he was propositioned by an older woman in a bar in Marbella soon after arriving in Spain. 'I was still with my girlfriend at the time – we were virtually engaged to be married – so I turned this woman down. But she slipped me her phone number, and when me and my girlfriend split up a few weeks later I called the woman up and agreed to sleep with her for money. It didn't seem such a big deal.'

Ninety per cent of his clients are English women, mainly rich divorcees all with one thing in common – a desire for the company of a younger man. And he insists that 'The sex is never a problem for me because I'm a randy sort of guy and up for anything, within reason. But you definitely need a good sense of humour in this game. The most important thing is to supply the women with exactly what they want. I always go on a date with an open mind.'

Deano says that the most popular request from his women clients is for oral sex. 'It seems that not many husbands bother to do this for their wives, but I'm more than happy to oblige. Why should men expect it from their wives but not give it to them back?' When Deano first started his job, he met another gigolo who gave him advice on certain aspects of his career. 'He told me to make sure I kept a note of all the clients' details in case there were any problems, and always to sort out the money before the sex. Now I always carry a pepper spray, but that's more to protect me from the husbands than the women themselves!'

The Costa del Crime has certainly provided Deano – as it has so many people featured in this book – with some quick-hit financial rewards. 'One woman wanted

me to take photos of her and me in bed together,' Deano
revealed, 'because it really turned her and her boyfriend
on. That particular woman initially paid me €50 for
meeting her plus €100 for sex; then she paid another
€400 for me to stay the night – six hours – with her in
bed. I've now put my rates up to €250 an hour plus
€600 for the night, and I've even got a website,
www.essexboys.com. The most I've ever earned from one
women was €4,000. She paid for all our entertainment
and meals, plus she gave me €600 for clothes during our
week together, and then there were the payments for the
sex. It was outrageous – she didn't even want to make
love all that often. I suppose you could call her my sugar
mummy. She was a very nice-looking English divorcee
aged 39 with a silver Mercedes. I went to her villa to
sleep with her. She used her husband's credit card to pay
for my clothes. She even wanted to know about me as a
person. She was interested in what I did, my girlfriends.
She's now become one of my regulars and we keep in
touch. I've even seen her out with her husband and
friends, although I'm always careful to pretend I don't
know her.'

Deano then revealed a hilarious gigolo scenario
featuring another 'professional' friend of his. 'This
Spanish guy who works with us, Antonio, had taken
Viagra for an afternoon job (a wife who just wanted an
hour in a hotel before her husband came home from golf)
and the job had gone as planned, but he just couldn't get
rid of his erection. He went straight home and played
solitaire [masturbated], but this didn't help either. He

used his belt to strap himself to his waist and walked to the bar to have a few drinks, hoping the alcohol would wear off the effects of the Viagra. He joined some friends, who were with a couple of girls at the time, but as he sat down his hard-on escaped from under his belt and, as he was wearing no underwear, poked out of the open fly of his trousers. The girls only caught a glimpse, but the friends who were sitting either side of him didn't know what to say! He sat there all night with his shirt pulled over himself, drinking twice as fast as everyone else in the hope that it would just go away.'

Like so many sex workers on the Costa del Sol, Deano leads two very separate lives. 'I sometimes bump into my own friends while I'm out working,' he explained, 'and when I tell them the woman I was with paid me for my company they think it's really cool. No one seems shocked or disgusted by what I do.'

Deano plans eventually to retire from being a gigolo and write a book about his experiences. 'But I'll probably write it as a novel so that I can change the names. Some of the heavy characters out here wouldn't be too pleased if I exposed their real identities.' He has already written up one typical encounter from his early days on the game. Here it is:

'Hi, I'm Deano.'

'Er, hello, I'm Marie. You're a little younger than I had expected, not that it really matters.'

'You said on the phone you just wanted sex, no talking, no going out, so...'

'Yes, yes. That's why it doesn't matter. Well, OK. Money, I suppose we discuss that first?'

'Yeah. You have the hotel room for the night, so to keep me here for that long is €400, but that's everything included.'

'I can't stay all night – my husband will be back from England in the early hours. What about two hours?'

'Well, that's €300 with everything.'

'OK. So, sorry to ask this, but how does it work? What I mean to say is, if I'm not satisfied, if I don't enjoy it or I don't come, do I get anything back?'

I really questioned my skills at that point and realised that the possibility of that hadn't even crossed my mind until that very moment. So without trying to sound arrogant I replied, 'Well, it hasn't happened yet so I don't know. But we can talk about it afterwards if you still feel the need.'

She raised her eyebrows and bit her lower lip while looking me up and down; the smile that followed the sex indicated I had laid her worries to rest. She gave me €400, and I stayed with her for another five hours.

On balance, Deano says, sleeping with women for money certainly beats living back in Essex. 'I'd probably have a nice safe nine-to-five job by now, but here there's always an element of excitement. I'll get back to normality eventually – but for the moment I couldn't be happier.'

CHAPTER TWENTY-THREE
PATRICK THE PIMP

Patrick on the streets – 'bitches'
not pictured

PATRICK THE PIMP

Patrick, in his well-polished Gucci loafers and neatly cut Armani suit, looks every inch the successful businessman. When you first meet him, the 30-year-old will tell you that he works in real estate. But beneath that charming, gold-toothed smile lies a cunning mind always on the lookout for the ultimate opportunity. As we walk up the narrow streets of the old centre of Marbella, his dark-brown eyes scan the faces and shapely bodies of every female who walks by.

'I can't help myself. I love women.'

If you think they sound like the words of a romantic man with a healthy interest in the opposite sex, you couldn't be more wrong: the 'real estate' in which Patrick specialises consists of apartments on the outskirts of Marbella occupied by some of the city's most beautiful prostitutes. Patrick is a pimp, and it's a career of which he is surprisingly open and proud. 'They're my bitches, and they don't do nothing without my permission,' he says without a hint of embarrassment. 'They all love me and will do anything I say. That's the way it's always been.'

Patrick has no doubt he's hit pay dirt by setting himself up as a pimp on the Costa del Sol. 'The girls come here from all over the world because there are so many rich men – and women – who want easy sex. I got English girls, Caribbean, South American, German, you name it. If you want something a little different like a trannie, I can put you in touch with the right people.'

All the more remarkable is that Patrick's girls really do seem to adore him. No doubt it might have something to do with the fact that he controls every aspect of their lives – they virtually cannot breath without his permission. The relationship between pimp and hooker might seem a curious one to somebody on the outside, but one of Patrick's girls explains it quite succinctly: 'I'm his bitch. He tells me what to do and I do it. I love him.'

But why? 'I can't help myself, I just do,' says an English girl called Lois from Bristol. 'I don't even accept that there's something unhealthy about my relationship with Patrick. All the men he introduces me to are just business, but when I sleep with Patrick it means something. I love him and would do anything for him.'

Another of Patrick's girls is 28-year-old Beatrice, a well-educated former teacher from Buenos Aires. 'I met Patrick in a bar on the seafront at Marbella. He bought me a drink and started chatting to me. He told me later he knew I'd make a good bitch because I come from a society where prostitution is not so disapproved of. I loved the way Patrick spoke to me. He made it all sound so normal, so easy, so natural. I was short of money, I needed a place to live and I didn't want to go back to Buenos Aires because there was nothing for me there,' explains Beatrice.

Just then Patrick interrupts with a sly smile. 'Tell them how nice I am, baby. How I look after you.'

A warm glow comes to Beatrice's face. 'It's true. I am proud to be Patrick's bitch. He gives me such a good life, why should I complain? I don't have to stand on any street corners, he pays for me to have health checks, and he's always in the apartment when men come by so I know I'm safe. What more could I ask?'

Patrick squeezes Beatrice's hand gently and they look into each other's eyes like a pair of young lovers. It's bizarre. Trying to get to the core of this extraordinary relationship, I ask him, 'If you love Beatrice so much, why do you let her sleep with so many other men?'

Patrick looks completely unfazed. 'That's just work, man. It don't mean nothing. My bitches know that I'm always there for them.' Looking straight into Beatrice's huge, saucer-like brown eyes, Patrick adds, 'Do I treat you bad, baby?'

Beatrice runs her hand up Patrick's leg and leans across to kiss him on the lips. Then she turns to me. 'I told you, I love him.'

How much drugs play a part in this relationship is anyone's guess, but the traditional form of control between pimp and hooker often revolves around narcotics. Patrick's extraordinary career began back in his birthplace, Holland, more than ten years earlier when he started running errands for a group of pimps in Amsterdam. 'But that place was too crowded, man. Some of the girls told me they were heading for Spain so I moved down here.'

Now Patrick's empire includes more than a dozen prostitutes, each in their own apartment. He reckons on making anything from €2,500 to €5,000 a week from the girls. On the day we met he was fixing up for six of his 'bitches' to entertain a visiting Arab sheikh who was staying at Marbella's most expensive hotel. 'This guy comes in once a year and his manager always calls me up to provide six of my best girls. They stay the weekend and he pays out €3,000 for each girl. That's good bread, man.'

Patrick looks on with a cold expression on his smooth-skinned face as Beatrice explains that 70 per cent of her customers don't even want to make love. 'They're into S&M, role-playing, latex, watching me having lesbian sex. It's really not so bad when you don't actually have to fuck the customers.'

Patrick then reels off the going rates for different forms of sex, like a second-hand-car salesman boasting about the prices of a whole range of vehicles. 'Oral, €200; lesbian, €500; whips, €700; full sex, €300...' He interrupts himself. 'That's for an hour, of course.'

But does Patrick have a normal, secret family life he's hiding from his bitches? It's not something he likes talking about it in front of one of his allegedly beloved girls. Later though, away from Beatrice, he confided, 'Sure, I got a wife and kids back in Holland. I don't see them so often these days, but I send them a lot of money.'

Patrick claims he rarely has problems with the local police. 'They know the score. Just as long as I keep the girls off the streets, they're happy. Sex is a big part of the attraction to tourists and foreign residents here, so they're not going to ban it, are they?'

He also claims that some of his best customers are British criminals who own houses on the Costa del Sol. 'I know some very heavy dudes who come down here with their families; sometimes they want a bit of fun so they call me up.' One notorious UK drugs baron recently contacted Patrick to provide a couple to make love in front of him and his wife. It was the perfect excuse for the pimp to mix work and pleasure. 'I don't normally join in, but on this occasion I got it together with one of my bitches in front of this dude while he and his wife watched. It was fun and he paid more than €2,000. Then he paid me another thousand to fuck his wife while he watched. It was cool. A good night's work.'

I swear I notice a slight look of jealousy on Beatrice's face as she listens to his sexual exploits. Patrick turns to her. 'It was only work, babe.'

Patrick prides himself on being a survivor, and insists he has a long-term plan to ease himself out of the business when the time is right. 'I like it down here, but

I know it won't last for ever. Other cats will come in and start taking my bitches from me. That's the way it is.' He believes that the apartments he has bought over the past few years and then 'lent' to his bitches will bring in a big profit when the time comes to sell them. 'I'm going to go into the real-estate market full time eventually. What I'm doing now is a young man's game. You got to know when it's time to move on, man.'

Patrick never actually uses the word 'pimp' during our conversations, but Beatrice inadvertently makes it crystal clear where the line is drawn. She asks Patrick, 'Can I go out to do some shopping later?'

Patrick takes a deep, slightly impatient breath. 'Not today, bitch. I got some clients for you.'

CHAPTER TWENTY-FOUR
DUNGEON QUEEN

Watch out, gentlemen, Ramona's
all out of dogs to walk

DUNGEON QUEEN

The hot weather, cheap liquor and many beautiful people make for a good time on the Costa del Sol. You just have to open the local weekly newspaper *SUR in English* and turn to the personal ads at the back to find hundreds of private and 'professional' people offering their 'personal services'. Whether you're gay, straight, bisexual, into threesomes, couples, single ladies, married ladies, guys, gals – you get the picture – you'll find what you're after in southern Spain.

Over in Puerto Banus, near Marbella, there are many bars where ladies and men of the night are available. Simply visit one of these taverns and you'll no doubt be approached by someone. Paying for sex in Spain can be cheaper than the rest of Europe: some prostitutes charge as little as €50. If you're a man with a fantasy about having sex with two women, then you can expect to pay around €150 for an hour or two. If it's a couple you're after – a man and a woman, that is – you can expect to pay the same or a little more, perhaps €200 for an hour or two.

It makes the Costa del Sol the perfect location for 38-year-old Ramona, who originally hails from Arizona in the good old US of A. She's a strong-willed woman with steely matt-black eyes that give little away. When she talks, it's machine-gun dialogue delivered at such a fast pace and with so little movement of the mouth that the words take a few moments to register. 'I love sex with men and women, old and young – but not underage, of course. I reckon I'm one of the few professionals who really does enjoy her job.' This is how Ramona starts our conversation in a spacious apartment overlooking a children's playground, a stone's throw from the Mediterranean in the centre of Fuengirola.

Ramona makes all aspects of sex sound so normal that you start to think that even the most perverse pleasures are thoroughly harmless. She describes herself as 'a mistress of pain and pleasure'. And no one would want to argue with her on that point. In a society where numerous men and women make money from sex, she genuinely gets off on what she does. 'I'm not some eastern-European girl forced into prostitution by a bunch of criminals against my will. I actually enjoy what I do and feel no shame about it either.'

During the week, Ramona entertains clients in her apartment where she charges €125 an hour for 'any type of sex I feel happy to perform'. Ramona is definitely the

one in charge. She even has a five-foot-high cage built in
the spare bedroom of her flat. 'I've got a couple of elderly
gentlemen who like being locked in their for twelve
hours at a time,' she says in a nonchalant tone of voice.
'They like begging me to let them out. One of them
even likes to clean the apartment naked. He pays me an
extra €500 for that pleasure. How many other people
get paid by their cleaner?'

Ramona arrived on the Costa del Sol from Arizona a
couple of years back. When I asked her what attracted
her to the area, she explained, 'I had a Mexican girl work
with me back in the States and she was always saying
how much more relaxed attitudes towards sex were over
here. I was getting hassled by the cops back in Arizona
on a daily basis, even though I wasn't breaking any laws
because I never had full sex with clients. But I knew it
was time to move on.'

Ramona eventually shipped over two crates of
equipment which, she boasts, prove she knows more
about sexual extremes than anyone else on the Costa
del Sol. 'I got everything from nipple clamps to colonic-
irrigation devices to master-and-slave rubber catsuits
and masks. There ain't nothing I haven't tried. Each to
their own, I guess. To tell you the truth, most of it's
worth trying at least once just to see if you enjoy it. I get
turned on to a lot of things that way.'

Within weeks of first arriving in Spain, Ramona began
advertising in swingers' magazines as well as more
traditional outlets such as the classified sections of the
local English-language newspapers. She soon found a

niche in the market. 'I quickly started building a good list of clients because I'm good at making sure that men lose their inhibitions. I'm not here to make them feel bad about themselves. I want them to enjoy themselves. That really turns me on.' Through the swingers' magazines, Ramona then tapped into a different type of market. 'I started holding regular Saturday lunchtime orgies with older couples. I didn't charge them anything because I considered that to be playtime. We soon got five or six couples turning up at the apartment. There was one wife – she still has a great body even though she's nearly sixty, I guess – and she would lie naked on the dining-room table while we all fondled and kissed her in turn. Then her husband would sit back and jack off while each of the men took it in turns to fuck her. She loved every minute of it and, I got to tell you, she always wanted more at the end.'

Ramona openly admits to being bisexual, although she says, 'I really prefer women because they know exactly how to turn me on.' Nor does she deny being a predatory type. 'If I see someone I want to have sex with, I make it really clear. I'll go up to a woman or a man in a bar and just ask them straight out if they want me. It's amazing how here in Spain no one seems shocked. It's like they're all thinking the same thing as well.' But she also has two favourite girlfriends with whom she spends a lot of time. 'I guess I sleep with them most nights, and they also work with me when I have a client who wants some type of orgy or S and M scene. It's much better to work with people you want to hang with.'

Ramona says she prefers British and German male clients 'because they seem to understand the point of sexual perversion. They don't treat me or my girls bad. They always have good manners and they truly seem to appreciate what we're doing for them. Spanish guys, on the other hand, treat us like cheap whores and that ain't nice. They also don't seem to understand how to get real kicks out of the darker stuff.'

Ramona sees herself as an artist. 'Listen, I put on a performance and if I come with a client it's a bonus. But the art is in satisfying that client.' Ramona is incredibly careful to have protected sex and insists that all clients wash and shower before any sexual activity. 'If a guy won't take a shower and use a condom, I show him the door.'

Only recently, Ramona recalled, three middle-aged British men visited the apartment and each took it in turn to have sex with her. 'It was fantastic. They were good-looking guys and had a fine, healthy attitude. I have to admit I really got off on having sex with them. They satisfied me in every sense of the word. And afterwards we all went out and had a meal at a local restaurant. They were real gentlemen.' It was only at the end of the meal that one of the men revealed to Ramona they were all serving police officers from the north of England. 'I scolded them for not bringing their uniforms with them!'

Ramona says her relationship with the local Fuengirola police department is good. 'They don't have a problem with me working here because I'm not out on the streets. That's where the police get angry because they don't like girls bothering tourists. I got one policeman who comes round here sometimes for some fun. But I have to pretend I don't realise he's a cop. Whenever I see him in the street he turns away from me. But I can live with it. A lot of guys don't like anyone knowing about their little sexual secrets. But hey, that's cool with me. It's part of the business. I like my customers happy, not sad.'

Ramona rarely has a day off, although she does sometimes like to relax on the nearby beach with a girlfriend and watch the world go by. 'I'm definitely a very sexual person, so sex is never far from my mind even as I'm lying there on the beach. If my cell phone goes off and it's a customer, I get a real turn-on from hearing their voice and knowing that in a short while I'll be back at the apartment having some fun.'

One of the most bizarre requests Ramona has ever had came at the beginning of last summer. 'I got a call from a guy I know in Marbella who said he had this friend who really wanted to meet me. He told me to go to this big villa on the beach near Puerto Banus and to bring my strongest whips and chains plus some really lethal-looking dildos and other stuff. He also told me only to wear a leather trench coat with nothing underneath. Wow, I was turned on just thinking about it! When I asked who the client was, my friend said it was just a businessman but that he was very rich and would pay €2,000. For that kind of money I was prepared to do more or less anything...'

But when Ramona got to the villa and her new client opened the door, she got a big surprise. 'It was this big Hollywood star – and I mean *big*. He didn't bat an eyelid, but just took me by the hand and led me into the open-plan sitting-room area. Inside were three of his male friends plus his wife. They were very polite, offered me a drink and then encouraged me to take all my equipment out of my case. Then I noticed all three men had unzipped themselves and the wife, who was not wearing panties, had lifted her skirt and was fondling herself.'

What followed was, in Ramona words, 'a full-blown orgy'. She explained, 'I'd be lying if I didn't say it was one of the most erotic experiences of my life. These guys did everything to me and then each took it in turn to service the wife. Then the movie star allowed me to beat him black and blue. We all eventually ended up in this huge king-sized bed sipping champagne and talking about what had happened as if it was the most ordinary thing you could imagine.

'To cap it all, I was given a thousand-euro tip. I felt so good when I left that villa I was tingling all over. Now every time I watch this guy in a movie I keep thinking about what he let me do to him and his wife!'

Like so many of the dodgy characters ducking and diving on the Costa del Sol, Ramona believes that she'll eventually make a fortune working the coastline and will be able to 'buy myself a nice *finca* in the mountains and disappear completely out of sight.'

She is very realistic about her professional future.

'Hey, I'm not getting any younger, and I know there'll be prettier, harder, hornier women soon trying to grab my business by promising to do things even I wouldn't go for. That will be when I take off and escape the rat race.'

Just then her mobile phone goes off. 'Sure, I can do that, honey.' She pauses. 'I'm going to hurt you, baby, hurt you real bad.' She flicks off the phone and turns to me. 'Got to get going, sweetheart. See you around...'

CHAPTER TWENTY-FIVE

NAUGHTY NIGHTSPOT

Going to the roadhouse to have a real good
time, somewhere near Fuengirola

NAUGHTY NIGHTSPOT

It might mean nothing to occasional visitors to the Costa del Sol but, for many of the area's dodgiest residents, there is a legendary nightspot. It is said that the prettiest girls in all Spain work there, and as such it attracts more criminals than probably any other establishment on the south coast.

Yet from the outside, any motorist could be forgiven for driving right past it without even realising it exists. Located between Fuengirola and Benalmadena on the old N340 coast road, which used to be the main route along the coast until the inland motorway finally relieved the traffic jams in the early-1990s, its reputation has spread far and wide in recent years. As one regular – a renowned drug baron originally from south-east London – told me, 'I don't know where they

214

get the girls from, but they're always really tasty and they don't hustle you too much either.'

First of all, a brief note of explanation for the uninitiated. Strictly speaking, it's illegal to run a brothel in Spain; but it's easy to get around the law by owning a bar attached to a 'hotel' where the girls take their clients. It's a well-used loophole, which politicians and police have ignored for years. As one Spaniard explained to me, 'Brothels have always thrived in Latino societies. There is a demand and they are considered completely normal. Men who use prostitutes are nothing unusual in this country. Prostitutes serve a useful purpose.' Many Spaniards point to the relatively small number of rapes and sex murders in their country as evidence that this attitude helps cut out such crimes. Others are not so convinced; they say that most wives and girlfriends are simply too scared in this macho society to make official complaints about such attacks to the police.

On any day of the month, it is said by many who frequent the club, you can walk into the dimly-lit bar area and find a woman with supermodel looks within five minutes. The girls in the club seem reasonably happy with their work. The ones from Brazil and other South American countries are driven by market forces to seek out the richer pastures of southern Europe. Other girls come from eastern Europe plus a handful from the UK and other northern European countries. Many of these prostitutes travel between brothels throughout Spain, changing location every few months.

Many of the women there, including beautiful blonde

friends Tanya, 23, and Denise, 25, from south London, prefer to work in pairs. 'It's always good to have one good mate when you work the clubs like us,' Tanya explains. 'You've got to have someone you trust because everyone around you is scum. It's the nature of the game.'

However, both girls agree that it is the best place to work on the whole Costa del Sol. 'Most of the guys who come in here know exactly what to expect,' says Denise. 'Sure, we get the occasional drunk who tries to cause trouble, but the doormen are usually very quick off the mark and they kick any troublemakers out within seconds.'

Step through the double doors of the club and you enter a twilight world where anything goes. Tanya explained the guidelines to me. 'None of us are allowed to tout for business. The men have to catch our eye and then start chatting to us. That keeps everything within the word of the law. What usually happens is you spot a fella and you know he's eyeing you up so you swing your hips past him and see if he says anything. The moment you get a proper reaction, you let him engage you in conversation.'

But it's not the conversation that attracts men here. Denise takes up the explanation: 'Normally, you spend a few minutes just chatting about where you're from, how long you've been in Spain, stuff like that. Then it's down to the nitty-gritty.'

'"How much?" is usually what comes next,' says Tanya. 'That's when you know you've hooked in a punter. I'd say that ninety per cent who ask that

question are going to end up in one of the rooms with
you within minutes. My going rate is €160 for an hour.
Most guys want pretty normal sex and if they want stuff
like oral I explain that they can have that during the
hour. But, like most of the girls here, we have our rules.
Neither of us would do anal. It's too risky for our health,
even with a condom.' She pauses before continuing.
'And you know what? A lot of the guys come before
they even get down to business, which makes life much
more pleasant for us.'

Tanya and Denise's speciality is performing lesbian
sex with a client watching. 'That's the option many girls
here prefer,' Tanya explains, 'because it usually doesn't
include penetration and nothing more than a bit of half-
decent acting.'

Denise reiterates what her friend means. 'Look, if me
and Tanya get it together for a fella it means not only
double the money but half the sex. Girls prefer not to be
alone with punters for obvious reasons – even in a hotel
room attached to the club something bad could happen.
This way, by offering a two-up, so to speak, a lot less
gets done. In any case, three quarters of the punters who
want a threesome are incapable of performing through
drink and drugs.'

Tanya and Denise also openly admit they 'have a
thing for each other', which means that being paid to
sleep together is usually 'a bit of a result'. 'Denise and I
are close to each other. We need each other to get
through working like this. We share a room together
when we're off duty and we've become very good

friends. We understand each other in and out of bed. It's a bit of bonus for the punters because when they ask us to perform together we actually sometimes get off doing it, which many girls don't. But the truth is that much of the time we just act sexy to keep the punters happy. We prefer doing things with each other in private.'

They insist they are not gay. 'I suppose we're both a bit bisexual,' admits Denise, 'but it's all about circumstance and we just happen to prefer each other's company at the moment. Doesn't mean we don't both want to one day find the man of our dreams and settle down and have kids and a nice home.'

But there is one golden rule, which is never broken. 'What is it?' I ask. Denise tells me. 'We never meet the punters outside of these premises. It would be madness, because you never know what might happen. I've heard stories about girls who've disappeared with rich punters and never been seen again. Apparently some were locked up as sex slaves, flown to Saudi Arabia and later killed. Stuff like that. It simply ain't worth the risk.'

One noticeable element missing from the mix in this brothel is the omnipresent pimp who seems to lurk in the shadows for so many working girls on the Costa del Sol. 'That's why so many girls come and work here,' Tanya explains. 'Pimps are evil bastards taking advantage of weak, needy girls. We certainly aren't like that, so this place is a real godsend. We're not making out this place is run by angels with only our best interests at heart, but at least the real scum – the pimps – are kept well away.'

It is rumoured that the management of the club insist on only a certain standard of girl working at the establishment. A Brazilian firecracker called Stella explained everything. 'There are rules about how we keep in shape and what sort of outfits we wear. Most of the girls wear platform shoes and skimpy bikinis, sometimes with stockings and suspender belts, but any girl who turned up here in an ankle-length skirt wouldn't be allowed into the club.'

Some of the eastern European girls who work here don't seem as sparky as girls like Tanya and Denise and the South American crew. One of them, a demure, dark-haired 21-year-old called Maria, from Bucharest, explained, 'It's much tougher for us because many of us have paid smugglers to get us here by ship or road. Then they keep our passports until we've paid our "fares". That's usually at least €3,000, which can take quite a while to earn in a place like this. It makes girls like us more timid and scared than the South Americans, most of whom have come here on their own.'

Maria, with her hunched shoulders and awkward manner, certainly doesn't exude confidence. 'Men have been horrible to me all my life and the men who come into a place like this are no better. Why should I trust any man after seeing what they do in here?'

Many of the eastern European prostitutes also end up sending much of their earnings back to their poverty-stricken relatives. 'It's a vicious circle. I feel really sorry for many of them,' says Tanya. 'Me and Den are just here to make as much cash as possible in a short period of time.

We call it a quick fix. But most of the girls from eastern Europe are going to be trapped here for years. It's not nice.'

The surprising thing about this club is that some men visit and simply order a drink, have a look at the talent on display, maybe chat with a girl for a few minutes and then depart. 'Often the Spanish guys come in here, order a drink, talk to one or two girls and then leave,' Tanya tells me. 'There's not such an air of desperation about them. They actually want to find a woman who suits them in almost the same way you might pick up a straight date in a normal bar. It's a different attitude. Often these sort of men are actually very nice to talk to. Sometimes a group of three or four of them will come into the club and stay all night chatting to the girls without actually hiring any of them for sex. The problem is that we don't make any money unless we use the attached hotel, so it's not exactly good for business.'

Tanya and Denise reckon there is a small number of girls working at the club who are on the lookout for a serious relationship. 'I know that some of the girls here hope that they can find themselves a rich guy who will set them up in a flat in Marbella, give them a credit card and a €2,000-a-month allowance and only expect the occasional bit of sex in return. Other girls have even married customers they've met in here. Me and Denise are definitely not on the lookout for that kind of man.'

At that moment Denise chips in. 'Look, we were just normal girls out on the pull back in the UK, but inside this place men only represent one thing to us: an instant payday. The decent, marriage types are out there in the real world. You can't combine business and pleasure. It don't make no sense.'

Meanwhile, life inside the club goes on. At any one time, more than 50 girls and an equal number of men are crammed into the main bar area. Strangely, the atmosphere is not nearly as repressive as one might imagine. There is a lot of laughing, even dancing and clinking of glasses. To a passing stranger it might even at first seem like a very friendly, ordinary bar until one studies the faces and bodies of the beautiful young women compared to their old and tired-looking male companions.

CHAPTER TWENTY-SIX
NATASHA THE LAPDANCER

When there's no poles to dance around, Natasha uses her head

NATASHA THE LAPDANCER

Natasha is just one of thousands of beautiful women who have turned up on the Costa del Sol to seek fame and fortune. Many end up working in the brothels and 'clubs' that provide prostitutes, but Natasha says she would never sell her body for sex. Instead, she's found a niche at a nightclub where the customers can look at girls, but definitely not touch them.

Natasha is a pole dancer. She's happy to gyrate and wriggle in front of an audience of men, often golfers who swamp the Marbella area all year round because of the good weather and numerous courses. As one of her bosses explains, 'Golfers tend to be cautious souls who travel in groups and fear that their friends might tell their wives if they visited a brothel, so many of them prefer clubs like this one where it's just a bit of good, old-fashioned, harmless fun.'

Natasha is 24 and comes from Latvia, and she agrees with her boss's explanation. 'I am not a prostitute and would never have sex with a man or woman for money. I am a professional dancer and I am very proud of my skills. In many ways I am an artist.'

Club customer Jim, from Northamptonshire, doesn't necessarily consider Natasha to be an artist as such, but at least he respects and appreciates girls like her. 'I'm here with some mates for a few rounds of golf. Of course, it's nice to pop into a club like this and look at the girls, but that's all we do. I'm not interested in hookers and nor are any of my mates. But it's certainly nice to unwind after a hard day's golf by having a drink and watching the girls dance.'

The Esta Noche nightclub in Marbella where Natasha and at least a dozen other girls dance each and every night is considered 'eccentric' by many local Spaniards. As one explained, 'In Spain, brothels are openly run. There is even one just a few hundred yards from Esta Noche, so it seems crazy to run a club where the men can only look at the women. What is the point?'

But staff at Esta Noche are convinced that the club has tapped into a previously unknown market. Says one manager, 'Look, guys coming here on golfing holidays don't all want to sleep with hookers. We're offering an alternative. What's wrong with that?'

Meanwhile, up on the club's stage, Natasha is wrapping her thighs around a pole and simulating sexual intercourse – in the nicest possible way, of course. She makes a point of looking deep into the audience, hoping to catch the eye of a wealthy punter who might then splash out €100 on a tip, or even buy a bottle of Dom Perignon and offer her a glass or two. But she insists that's definitely where she draws the line.

Natasha is then joined on stage by Fran from Derbyshire. She's a buxom blonde who turned up on the Costa del Sol a few months earlier after plying her trade at one of London's best-known pole-dancing clubs, just off Oxford Street in the West End. 'It's much nicer out here,' she tells me. The people are cooler than they are back home. We don't have any problems with pig-headed customers who think all the girls are just easy lays.'

Fran lives in the same apartment block in nearby Fuengirola as her friend Natasha. They are small studio flats, but both girls say their standard of living has greatly improved by being on the Costa del Sol. 'Back in Latvia I lived at home with my mother,' Natasha tells me, 'unable to afford to move out because my job in a factory barely paid me enough to afford to even go out more than once a month.' Now she has an English boyfriend whom she hopes to marry one day, and she believes her career as a pole dancer will provide far more opportunities in the long term. 'Look, I work relatively short hours. I earn a thousand euros a week and I can send some of that back to my mother. I am very happy here.'

Since starting dancing at Esta Noche in 2002, Natasha has concluded that the kind of men who frequent such clubs are 'basically good people. They respect us as women and that makes this job a lot easier.' But does her English boyfriend mind her working at such an establishment? 'He's not that happy about it, but he knows I would never go with any of the customers. He wants me to get a nice office job, but accepts that will not happen for a few years yet.'

However, working from 8pm until 4am does play havoc with Natasha's social life. 'Obviously I have little time to make new friends. I don't tend to get up until about twelve midday and I have to leave here for work at seven each evening.' Natasha uses much of her spare time painting pictures of ... nude women! 'I am fascinated by the human body and, by painting pictures of naked people, I find myself trying to perfect my skills as an artist.' Friends have told Natasha she has genuine talent as an artist, and she hopes one day to persuade a local gallery to hold an exhibition of her work. But she is very realistic about her artistic future. 'I know I will probably never make a living from my paintings, but I feel very lucky to be able to dance and paint. It's a wonderful combination.'

Surprisingly, some of Esta Noche's customers are female. 'It might surprise many people, but we get women coming in here too. Some of them are in hen parties passing through, but there are a number of regular female customers who come here at least once a week.' Natasha believes that some of them are genuinely interested in studying the girls' dance techniques. But she does admit that 'Some of the older women are definitely gay or bisexual, and they often try to chat the girls up between dances.'

Natasha even recalled how one rich businesswoman returned to the club five nights in a row after sharing a bottle of champagne with her. 'She was a very elegant older woman, probably in her late forties. I accepted a drink with her and sat at her table the first night she came to the club. She obviously had a crush on me and kept touching my leg under the table, but I did not react and eventually she stopped trying to touch me and seemed to accept that I was not gay. But then she came back the following four nights and got very upset when I wouldn't sit down with her at the table again. She even sent me a note asking me to meet her after the club closed, but I ignored it. Then on the fifth night, as I was leaving the club, she got out of a chauffeur-driven limousine and tried to persuade me to go to her hotel with her. I refused as politely as possible, but she got very angry and started shouting at me and calling me names. Luckily one of the club managers came out at that moment and calmed things down. I'd never realised until then that women can be just as aggressive as men if they want sex.'

Natasha is completely anti-drugs and insists that she drinks only in moderation. 'I prefer to stay in control so that nothing bad can happen to me. It's better that way.' She even keeps a glass bottle, shaped like a stiletto shoe, filled with potent Latvian liqueur, untouched by her bed as a reminder of what alcohol can do. 'That drink is the key to everyone's unhappiness where I come from, and keeping that sealed bottle makes sure I never forget the harm it can cause.' Both Natasha and Fran admit the probability that most nights many of the customers are on drugs. 'It's obvious from the way they behave. But in my opinion, they are stupid because drugs make you more vulnerable. I only enjoy this job because I am sober all the time.'

The dancer is full of praise for the British management of the club. 'They have created a real family atmosphere. I feel I can talk to them about any problems I have without worrying that they will fire me. Also, most importantly, they never put us under any pressure to be extra nice to the customers. Sure, some of the men and women who come here flash a lot of cash at us, but that doesn't mean we have to like them all, does it?'

Only recently, a famous English Premiership soccer star visited the club with some friends. 'I didn't even know who he was until one of the English girls recognised him,' Natasha admits. But the star, renowned for his nightclubbing antics in London, soon focused all his attention on Natasha. 'I was dancing my favourite routine to Gary Glitter's 'Rock'n'Roll' when I got this spontaneous burst of applause. I looked down and it was this soccer player and his friends. I smiled at them – but that was it – and just carried on dancing.' However, Natasha did admit that, 'To be honest about it, I was flattered by his attention and I made sure my next dance routine was extra sexy, but that's just having a bit of fun as far as I am concerned.'

However, the soccer star took Natasha's sexy dance routine a little too literally. 'As I finished, he gave me this huge round of applause. It was a bit embarrassing. A few minutes later in the changing rooms, one of the waitresses brought me an envelope. I opened it to find it contained a thousand euros and a note asking me to meet him at his hotel later. I sent the letter and money back to him. The waitress said he looked very disappointed when he got the envelope back, but insisted she take me back the money as a tip even though I was refusing to meet him. At least he was a gentleman. I've heard a lot of horror stories from girls about other guys.

'I guess I've been lucky compared with so many other girls who've come to the Costa del Sol. I've got a decent job. No one is trying to exploit me. I have a boyfriend who one day I hope to marry. They aren't many girls like me out here who can say the same, are there?'

CHAPTER TWENTY-SEVEN
TRANNIE VALERIE

Stepping out, Valerie offers the best
of both worlds

TRANNIE VALERIE

Down on the Costa del Crime, it's not just the boys and girls who provide the sexual services that so dominate this sandy coastline. There is a big demand for ladyboys too. These *travesti* – as they're called in Spain – walk a bizarre line between the two sexes but retain much fascination for many men *and* women.

Valerie, 28, is a classic example of this ever-growing trade. In her husky voice she discusses in detail what it is about her that attracts such interest. 'Most of my clients are men, but very few of them are gay. I find it very fulfilling because I am not interested in girls: I am only attracted to straight men, the more masculine the better.

'Many married men go to a transsexual prostitute because they believe they are not committing adultery as we are not real women in their eyes,' she explains. 'It might seem a strange attitude, but it is true.'

Valerie also claims that the popularity of transvestite hookers in Spain and South America is based on the regions' history of Catholicism. 'We can't get pregnant, can we?' she says, with a look of genuine seriousness on her face.

Many of the transsexuals and transvestites based on the Costa del Sol hail from South America where it seems there is a huge she-male community. Valerie, on the other hand, comes from the south-east of England, although she has Indian parents. She has been working in Spain for nearly three years and says that she's been surprised by the respect and gentleness shown towards her by nearly all her clients. 'As a schoolboy back in Britain, I lived my life struggling to survive despite being very effeminate. I was teased at school and did badly as a result. I was beaten black and blue regularly. Life was, frankly, horrible.

'When I told my parents at the age of sixteen that I wanted to take hormone shots and start dressing as a girl, they were horrified. They tried to stop me ever leaving the house, and for a while I became a complete hermit, unable to travel anyway because I didn't have the money to buy any women's clothes.'

The breakthrough for Valerie – she refuses to reveal her previous identity – came when she went to her GP, who immediately recommended treatment on the National Health Service. 'It was such a relief to meet someone who understood what I was going through.' But then she changed her mind about having an operation to remove her penis. 'I suppose the truth is I was terrified of the operation. I had started to develop breasts thanks to hormone treatment, and the natural next step was to have surgery. But I couldn't go through with it.'

Eventually, the NHS treatment came to an end and Valerie was left neither a man nor a woman in the eyes of herself or other people. 'At first I shrank back into my little shell at home, never going out but at least able to continue dressing as a female. I grew my hair and started to wear make-up every day, but then my parents disowned me and threw me out of the house. I had nowhere to go and no friends in the world, so I ended up living in a squat in east London. It was a horrible time for me. I wanted to kill myself and came very close to doing so. I was turning tricks in alleyways but it was a horrible existence. I was lucky I didn't catch AIDS.'

Valerie says she then met another transsexual named Debbie, who had once been a highly educated university professor called Michael from a rich family. He had also been disowned in similar circumstances. 'Debbie taught me a lot about self-respect – how I had to fend for myself and stop relying on others. She snapped me out of my depression, self-loathing and self-pitying behaviour. We became the very best of friends.'

After months of living on the dole, both Valerie and Debbie decided to travel to the Costa del Sol. 'We'd met a few South American transsexuals in London and they kept saying how much more relaxed attitudes were in southern Spain. Since it wasn't that far away it seemed a good idea to start a new life here.'

But just a few months after arriving in the Estepona area, Debbie died in a road accident. 'I was devastated, but I kept remembering how Debbie had pulled me out of my problems in London and I decided to keep my life together for her sake more than anything. I was determined to survive.'

Valerie eventually started working at a brothel near Estepona that specialised in transsexual prostitutes. 'It wasn't like working the streets back in London. The clients treated us like real people, not freaks to be kicked and abused. The madam who ran the brothel was a good person who genuinely cared about us. She made sure we had regular health checks, and paid us a decent cut from every customer. She looked after me like a mother.' Wouldn't she have liked a safe, secure nine-to-five job in a normal environment? 'In a perfect world, I suppose so, but I had to be realistic and face the fact that it was not going to happen.'

Valerie worked at the brothel until 2003 when she decided to set up business on her own by advertising in the classified section of a Costa del Sol English-speaking newspaper. 'I think I probably have fewer problems with clients than straight hookers because the men who come to me know exactly what to expect. I've built up a good working relationship with a number of regular clients who visit me most weeks. Many of them are British and they always seem so relieved that I am English. I think it makes them feel more relaxed.'

Valerie believes that more than 50 per cent of her clients are married. 'But that doesn't make them gay or bad husbands,' says Valerie. 'I think what I offer is something different. A change of scenery, if you like. Where's the harm in that? It's a free world, after all.'

But the biggest revelation to Valerie about living on the Costa del Sol is the attitude towards transgendered people such as herself. 'I often go out dressed up in my favourite skirt, blouse and boots and I feel so much more confident here in Spain because, although some people probably know I am a transsexual, they don't treat me like some freak. They are warm and friendly towards me.'

Valerie says she has many girlfriends who are constantly asking her to help them out with relationship problems. 'I think maybe because of my masculine side they feel that I can give them better advice than other women. It's very rewarding to be needed after years and years of being a social outcast.'

Valerie says she even has 'a special man friend'. 'I met him professionally at first, but he asked me out for dinner one night and our relationship has turned into something quite serious. He's so nice and gentle and understanding, and even takes me out shopping at weekends. He doesn't seem to care when people sometimes look strangely at us. He's been married twice and feels very reluctant to get into another relationship, but says that I make him feel really wanted for the first time in his life. It's a very rewarding relationship for me.'

But Valerie says it is unlikely in the foreseeable future that she will ever retire from the vice game. 'It's an obvious career for me, but that's exactly how I look at it

– as a career. I don't often enjoy the sex with clients. In that way I suppose I am a lot like a straight hooker; but I have to make a living to survive, and there is plenty of demand for me on the Costa del Sol.'

Valerie is extremely strict about what she will and will not do for clients. 'I have very strict rules about cleanliness, anal sex and lots of other areas that I don't want to talk about here. Just because I am a prostitute doesn't mean I don't have feelings. There are definitely times when I just grin and bear it as a man has sex with me. Often the biggest problem is having an erection. If I was a complete woman it would be so much easier to pretend that I was excited. You see, it's not as easy or as blatant as you think!'

Nearly all Valerie's clients like her to be as feminine as possible. 'It's almost as if they don't want to even guess what my real sex is, even though I have a penis hanging down in front of their eyes. Most men adore me to wear stockings and sexy underwear and lots of make-up with high heels. Some clients even complain if I have a little stubble – I don't blame them!'

CHAPTER TWENTY-EIGHT
TWO BEST FRIENDS

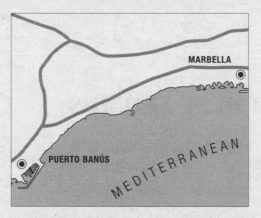

All the way to Puerto Banus, Jenny and her
friend Madonna. From Kent

TWO BEST FRIENDS

Bubbly blondes Jenny Fairchild and her best friend Madonna Thompson, from Kent, arrived on the Costa del Sol determined to spend at least two years in the sunshine. They worked as part-time models back in Britain, and thought they'd be able to get similar jobs in the thriving local film and TV commercials industry.

'We went to loads of castings but never got one job,' explains 23-year-old Jenny. 'Then there was the language. We couldn't speak a word of Spanish and a lot of the jobs were for Spanish TV. It was a nightmare. Our next big mistake was that we'd got ourselves a short-lease flat in Malaga, which is a busy city, not a resort. Not that many people spoke English. It turned out to be a disaster.'

Madonna, 24, adds, 'We was getting really depressed. It was costing a lot more to live out here than we'd bargained for and we started feeling really desperate. Trouble was we didn't want to go home either. There was nothing for us in Kent so we got drunk one night and decided we'd do *anything* to survive.'

The girls then met a 'right dodgy German' called Hermann in a bar, who suggested they might like to work in his club in the centre of Malaga. 'He was a right creep so we turned him down,' says Jenny. 'But I kept his phone number and a few days later when we were down to our last twenty quid we decided to give him a call.'

Both girls knew that the 'club' run by Hermann was 'probably a bit sleazy'. 'But we just presumed it was the type of place where you get the punters to buy an expensive bottle of bubbly and then they give you a nice big tip,' explains Madonna.

But the moment they walked into the club, located in a narrow side street near Malaga's main port area, both girls realised they were entering a brothel. 'We stopped for a moment and I looked at Jen. "Well, you on for this?" I asked her.

'She just shrugged her shoulders. "In for a penny, in for a pound." So in we went. We didn't have a lot of choice in the matter. We reckoned that, just as long as we stuck together, we'd be OK.'

The two girls had been promised free accommodation by Hermann when he asked them to come and work for him. They were literally living above the shop, and this club was a long way from the vast whitewashed haciendas and luscious golden sandy beaches of nearby resorts like Marbella and Puerto Banus. 'We were right in the middle of a big-city port, and some of the men that came into that club were pigs off visiting ships. Many were eastern European seamen who were smelly, unshaved and mean with their money. It was bloody awful,' remembers Madonna.

The first night in the seedy club, both girls were so scared that they couldn't bring themselves even to talk to the customers. Jenny described the scene to me. 'It was very dimly lit in the club and it just made all these men look even more scary. Madonna and I just huddled together in a corner, afraid to talk to anyone.' Within a couple of hours, Hermann pulled the girls into his side office and yelled at them for not mixing with the customers. 'He was furious and kept shouting at us. Then he said that unless we both slept with him in an upstairs room that night he'd chuck us out on the street. It was a nightmare. We begged him for another chance because we had nowhere else to turn.'

Jenny and Madonna say that they both then reluctantly agreed to the German's sexual demands because at least he was clean and used a condom. 'It wasn't pleasant,' Madonna admits, 'but it was better than having to sleep with his customers.'

For the following month, they lived in a tiny bedroom and 'serviced' Hermann. 'He said we didn't have to sleep with the customers,' Jenny told me, 'just so long as we went with him. We dreaded every knock on the door of that little bedroom because it was always him. He wouldn't even let us leave the room between eight in the evening and eight in the morning because he liked to come upstairs and visit us whenever he felt the urge.' He called the girls his concubines. They didn't even know what the word meant until Jen looked it up in a dictionary.

After a month of virtually round-the-clock sexual degradation, Jenny and Madonna felt completely trapped. 'He paid us nothing, but gave us free accommodation, drink and food. We had nowhere to turn,' says Madonna.

Then Hermann tried to persuade the two girls to sleep with another man who worked in the bar of the club. It was the last straw for Jenny and Madonna. 'It was only then we realised that he was trying to become our pimp. He told us this man was going to come up to our room and we would have to sleep with him otherwise he'd chuck us out. That was it. We both agreed enough was enough and packed our bags and made a run for it.'

Jenny and Madonna caught a late-night bus up the coast to the Marbella resort of Puerto Banus. 'We didn't know what else to do. I'd earlier met one guy in a bar who'd said that many English-speaking girls made a good living picking up men in bars in Puerto Banus where there were lots of rich people.'

The two British girls headed for the Burger King, changed into their tightest Lycra dresses and highest heels in the toilets, and then tottered out towards the numerous bars and clubs alongside the marina area, which was filled with dozens of multi-million-pound yachts. 'Before we'd even got to any of the bars,' Jenny told me, 'these two good-looking British guys approached us and asked if we wanted to have a drink with them. They were nice, polite, middle-aged men – not like the animals inside that Malaga club.'

Within an hour Jenny and Madonna had struck a deal to go back to the men's hotel and stay the night. 'They agreed €750 each,' reveals Jenny. 'It was a fortune to us. It was like a dream come true after all we'd been through.'

'This was a completely different ball game,' continues Madonna. 'The hotel was beautifully decorated and the men we went with were real gentleman. Turned out they were in Puerto Banus for some work conference. Both of them seemed to be loaded.'

That first experience convinced Jenny and Madonna that they should specialise in picking up rich clients in Puerto Banus nightclubs and bars. 'We always stuck together as a pair because it made us feel safer,' explains Madonna.

In their first two weeks, both girls say they earned €5,000 each. It was the height of the season and the place was heaving with wealthy men. But the honeymoon period didn't last long. Jenny takes up the story. 'One night, a man we met in a bar who was a well-known local British drug dealer persuaded us to go with him to a party in a villa up in the hills behind Marbella. Turned out to be twenty British men in that house and they all wanted to have sex with us. We refused and they got really heavy with us. Three of them then tried to rape Madonna. She managed to break free and we ran out of the villa. The drug dealer phoned us the next day, screaming and shouting and threatening to kill us for not having sex with his friends. We were so scared we moved out of our new apartment in case they came round and got us.'

Jenny and Madonna then started work at a well-known brothel in San Pedro, just off the main N340 coastal road towards Estepona. 'It was like a cattle market in there, but at least they gave us a room to stay in when we were off duty. The hours are tough. It's 6pm until 6am, but we both feel safer in this environment. Many of the customers who walk into the club looking for sex are British holidaymakers. A lot of these men even sneak out of their hotels leaving their wives and kids asleep and unaware that they've gone off to a brothel. It takes all sorts, I guess.'

Jenny and Madonna both insist they will quit the brothel once they have earned enough cash to set themselves up as dominatrixes in a decent apartment in Marbella. Says Madonna, 'We reckon that running a dungeon would be much better because then we don't have to have actual sex with the clients. This club is a real strain because some nights we have to go with more than half a dozen men. We charge them an average of €150–200 each, so the money's good even though we have to give thirty per cent of that to the manager of the hotel attached to the bar. But at least none of the clients can beat us up or anything like that, because everything happens on the premises.'

Both girls claim they gained good A-level grades at

school back in Britain and had both originally applied to work as flight attendants based at Gatwick Airport. 'But we got turned down,' explains Jenny, 'because we'd both been nicked as kids for shoplifting. If it hadn't been for that, none of this would have happened to us. Doesn't seem fair, does it?' They insist they 'aim to go straight eventually and get ourselves jobs as reps or something like that.' Yet they are both adamant that they prefer working in a brothel to being back in England. 'Most people we know are stuck in boring jobs in banks and stuff like that. Others are out of work. I'm not proud of being a hooker, but we've both managed to get through it by detaching ourselves from the reality of what we're doing. It's not that hard.'

Madonna has the final word. 'I think it's true to say that both our attitudes towards sex have changed since we got here. We know there are bad people out there who could hurt us but we've grown up very quickly and we both reckon we can now handle ourselves. You see, there are good and bad people everywhere in the world. We just need to make sure we know how to spot the bad 'uns.'

CHAPTER TWENTY-NINE
COSTA DEL SILICONE

Floating to a better body the
Spanish way

COSTA DEL SILICONE

There is another controversial business thriving on the Costa del Sol. It attracts a wide range of customers, but they all have two specific aims: to look beautiful in old age and to improve their sex lives. The south of Spain has become a plastic-surgery paradise for the over-50s. Each year thousands of people book into clinics in Marbella and other similar establishments, returning home with wrinkles smoothed and sagging faces reshaped.

Back in the early-1990s, most of the patients would fly over from the UK for their nips and tucks; but now that UK residency in the Costa del Sol has increased tenfold over the past five years, the number of locally based patients has shot up. As one clinic director explains, 'A lot of women come here telling their husbands they're going on a shopping trip with a female friend and then go home and say they've had a new hairdo. Some men would be furious if they knew – how dare they spend money like that! – but most, after thirty years of marriage, don't even notice. Why tell him, if he would only go mad and think she was doing it for another man?'

A number of Costa del Sol clinics hold initial cosmetic consultations for tourists back in London at which measurements and photographs are taken. If they decide to go ahead, they're collected from Marbella Airport and taken straight to the clinic for a full medical before the operation.

The clinic director I spoke to usually tends to recommend what he calls the lower facelift, which involves tidying the neck and chin. It is the most popular operation and the easiest to pass off once the patient gets home. 'It doesn't alter the face like a full facelift. Ladies who don't want their husbands to know can easily get away with it.'

These secretive jobs are getting ever more popular. Privacy at the clinic is all important. After an overnight stay at the Hospital Europa in Marbella, clients are transferred to rooms at a modest local three-star hotel near the centre of the old town. Cosmetic-surgery patients have taken over the entire top floor of the building. As the swelling subsides and the bruises fade, clients emerge with eyes hidden behind dark glasses. In the evenings they cluster at dimly lit local tapas bars, confident that no one they know will spot the tell-tale stitches or the scars behind their ears.

One woman I spoke to in Marbella admitted to having

returned three times for similar operations; now in her early 60s, she says this may be her last attempt at an overhaul. The elegant former air hostess told me, 'Age can be very cruel to somebody who has been beautiful. I look at photos of myself forty years ago and gasp. Did I really look like that? Having an operation is my way of at least making myself feel half as confident as I did back then.'

Among the Brits of the Costa del Sol who have recently gone under the scalpel are two well-known TV actresses and one renowned Scottish comedian. But these patients are extra bashful, afraid that if their fans knew their cosmetic secrets, their careers will be over.

One elegant peroxide blonde, on holiday in Marbella with a girlfriend, says she was delighted by the neck and jawline lift that had just cost her £5,000. She even insists she had told her husband back in Sussex. 'But I try not to tell many friends because people in general seem to have this appalling attitude towards cosmetic surgery, which I think is entirely unfair.' However, this very savvy lady does admit that she pretended to her husband that the operation had cost half of what it actually did. 'I sent the clinic one early cheque stating "in full and final settlement" and only showed that to him,' she says proudly. 'He was none the wiser.'

But does all this surgery, combined with a wonderfully bronzed body, improve the sex life? One lady who has had a nose job at another clinic near Estepona is adamant. 'Yes! My husband still only manages to perform once a month, but I've found myself a wonderful Spanish toy boy who likes to make love three times whenever I see him, and that's usually for a couple of hours in the evening, twice a week.'

Almost half of the clinics' patients are men who seem to be equally capable of subterfuge. Terry, from the Marbella resort of Nuevo Andalucia, still sports a ponytail and plenty of bling bling, even though he has just celebrated his 60th birthday. 'I still love pulling birds, so splashing out six grand on a facelift was definitely a good investment for me. I feel ten years younger and the type of women I've met recently has definitely improved. I'm in good shape.'

Terry opted for a quick nip and tuck after his third marriage to a much younger woman hit the rocks. 'The singles game out here is tough. More and more younger blokes are trying to pull the richer, older women. By having a facelift, I've upped the ante and it's working well.'

Meanwhile, the clinic director has no doubt that the number of patients will continue to increase. He even claims to have pioneercd the so-called lunchtime mini-facelift. He is an unashamed salesman for cosmetic surgery and he considers himself to be the ultimate professional. Operations at his clinic are carried out by a highly respected Spanish professor.

He insists it's the men who have more sob stories than the women. 'Men tell me they're on the scrap heap at sixty. They would do anything to find work and survive. Then they have a facelift and take ten years off their CV. You can't stop the clock, but you can slow it down. People age through stress, or because they're treated abominably by their partners. Some patients' stories break your heart.'

Lisa and Georgina, who live on the same urbanisation in Estepona, both had operations recently. Both women are in their 50s. Lisa's husband died two years ago. 'I lost all confidence and didn't leave the house for eighteen months after he died. Then I decided to have surgery to rejuvenate myself both physically and mentally. I realised I couldn't let my life just end because of his death. It's turned out to be the best thing I've ever had done. I feel confident for the first time in years. My husband would turn in his grave if he knew I'd been under the knife!'

Her friend Georgina had cheek implants to contour a round, flat face. 'I didn't do this just to try and pull younger men,' she says bluntly. 'It's about self-esteem. I'm not that interested in a new relationship. I'm divorced and my last husband showed me that men in general are pigs. But I do admit I enjoy teasing them more now when they try and pick me up in bars.'

A facelift is far from simple. This is what is involved in a full facial 'overhaul':

1. Complete forehead lift, repositioning and lowering of hairline.
2. Upper and lower eye bags removed.
3. Nose reshaped; stitches dissolve internally.
4. Nose-to-mouth area shortened.
5. Fat taken from thigh to make lips fuller.

6. Silicone chin implant; stitches dissolve inside
   mouth. Loose skin removed from neck and jawline;
   muscles repositioned for longer-lasting result.

As the husband of one woman who spent more than
£10,000 on cosmetic surgery explained, 'I was shocked
when I heard how much it cost, but the results are
fantastic. It's like she's a new, younger woman to look at
and she's suddenly started making pretty outrageous
sexual demands as well! I think the ops have unlocked
her character, allowed her to be herself for the first time
in years. It's certainly rejuvenated our marriage.'

And the woman herself said, 'Once I started talking
about having it done, I was surprised how many of my
friends had already had bits and bobs done. Others said,
"Go for it. If you look good, we'll do it too." Only my
youngest daughter was worried. She kept asking me,
"You'll still have a nice smile, won't you?" But I
definitely feel my face is still my own; it's not a mask.
Now my confidence has returned and I feel I'm really
back in the world. I keep looking in the mirror and
thinking, "Is that me?" I don't care who knows I've had
a facelift when it looks so wonderful.'

CHAPTER THIRTY
PORNO DEL SOL

It's location, location, location, as 'Grubby
Vic' makes his flicks along the coast

PORNO DEL SOL

One of the Costa del Sol's most notorious porn-film-makers is a 59-year-old Brit with bleached hair called, rather predictably, 'Grubby Vic'. He's a remarkably straightforward character, considering the dubious nature of his business: he sees it simply as a matter of supply and demand. 'I knock out the porn and the punters buy it by the bucketful. Is that so bad?'

It is typical of Grubby to play down his role as the ultimate purveyor of porn on the southern coast of Spain. He started in the film business more than 40 years ago when he worked as a camera assistant on some of those classic old *Carry On* comedies, starring stalwarts Barbara Windsor, Syd James and just about every other light-entertainment icon of the 1960s. As Grubby explains, 'The pay was rubbish, but we had a right laugh – although I knew the producers were doing very well, leaving the rest of us struggling.'

It wasn't long before Grubby and a couple of his pals from the camera crew decided to branch off into their own 'specialised' side of the film business. 'I knew there must be a market for porn films, but back in them days there was no video so it was an expensive business putting together a movie. I contacted an old boy I knew who owned a few strip clubs in the West End of London. He got together a few grand, persuaded his favourite girls to appear for free and off we went.'

Grubby admits that those early efforts 'weren't up to much, but they made the rounds in all the dirty bookshops because there wasn't anywhere else you could sell porn back in them days.' Then he had the brainwave of advertising his 'saucy movies', as he called them, in the personal pages of *Exchange and Mart*. 'Suddenly I had more customers than hot dinners. What was surprising was that so many people had their own home movie projectors to play the films. I made all the investor's money back for him and even managed to keep a few bob for myself.'

But for the following ten years, Grubby struggled to make a full-time living out of the burgeoning porn-movie business. 'I was also blacklisted by the so-called legit British film industry; at around the same time the UK film business collapsed. So not only was I not allowed near a film set, but most of my mates were on the dole. It was a difficult time.'

Then Grubby got himself a job running one of those

very same Soho bookshops. He also fronted a couple of hostess clubs for one of the most evil West End porn barons of the 1970s. 'It was a funny old time back then. We had loads of coppers in our pocket and the filthy mags were flying off the shelves at a rate of knots, but the porn-film business had stalled. It was just too tricky to make a decent movie that people would buy.'

Then along came the 1970s porn classic *Deep Throat*; suddenly Grubby and his merry men were back in demand. 'But it was the invention of the video that made all the difference. *Deep Throat* and a load of other Californian porn films were initially shown in backstreet flicks; once they got released on video people started flocking to buy them.'

Grubby Vic was not one to let such obvious opportunities slip through his hands. 'I taught myself how to handle one of the earliest video cameras. It was a huge great thing and weighed a ton, but once we'd shot the pictures that was it. We didn't have to do all that long-winded processing that you had to go through with reels of old-fashioned film.'

Needing good weather to shoot an outdoor porn film about life in a nudist holiday camp that had the endearing title of *Love in a Warm Climate*, Grubby headed out to southern Spain and borrowed a criminal associate's villa near Marbella to shoot his movie. 'It was late October and I wanted the film ready for the Christmas market, so I was delighted to find it sunny and eighty degrees when I got out there.' He has never looked back. 'I knew it was the place for me the moment the plane touched down at Malaga Airport. Lots of pretty birds everywhere, plenty of geezers prepared to get at it in front of a camera. I never had to recruit any more actors from England. This was where it was at.'

From the late-1970s onwards, Grubby reckons he shot an average of ten porn movies a year. 'They don't have a long shelf-life. Back in them early days, it was all pretty straight stuff. I used to recruit women and men from local clubs and by putting advertisements in the classified sections of the Costa's English-speaking newspapers. We never did much other than straight sex and a bit of oral. Back then we didn't even like to show actual dicks. It was pretty tame stuff by today's standards.'

But Grubby's arrival on the Costa del Sol coincided with the influx of British criminals taking advantage of the lax extradition treaty between the UK and Spain. 'A lot of heavy fellows turned up on my doorstep wanting a piece of my porn-film business. They couldn't accept that I was running a straight business and the last thing I needed was a bunch of bored old bank robbers with nothing else to do but cause me a load of aggro. That's what often happens out here when villains want somewhere to launder their cash. Most of them didn't have the skills to knock out their own movies so they tried to muscle in on my set-up, but I somehow managed to see them off without any real problems.'

From the late-1970s through to the mid-1980s, Grubby says he continued knocking out porn videos, but then came demands for more varied types of movies.

'The punters no longer wanted to just watch a pretty couple in their mid-twenties getting it together by the side of a luxury swimming pool in the sunshine. I was being asked for more specialist material, like S and M, orgies, bisexual stuff, even some gay material.'

Ever the adaptable professional, Grubby started franchising off some of his work to other supposed film-makers on the Costa del Crime. 'It was a recipe for disaster. I started working alongside some right cowboys who didn't know one end of a camera from a Hoover. We wasted a lot of cash on rubbish product and meanwhile others were flooding the market with anything-goes material, which was pretty explicit. I used to take a week knocking out a decent porn film, all shot at one house with lots of set-ups featuring at least five different women and three men. But these arseholes were trying to do it all in a two-day shoot. As the quality started to deteriorate, so did the demand. The punters knew they were being conned and turned their backs on us.'

Then Grubby discovered that one of his cowboy partners had raped an actress in front of the rest of his camera crew and threatened to kill anyone who reported him to the police. 'That was completely out of order. This animal even pulled a gun on me in a row over what he'd done. That was when I realised I had to pull out of the business until things cooled down. I didn't want to be associated with a bunch of sick bastards like that.'

Grubby also discovered that, by producing 'softer' edits of his films, he could exploit TV outlets in hotel rooms and at regular video stores. 'So I stopped making

260

them and simply got out all the old ones and re-edited them to make them acceptable for these so-called "normal" outlets. It was a licence to print money. My films were soon being shown in hotel chains across the world, and even Blockbuster was stocking them.'

With four marriages under his belt and 'an assortment of kids here and back in London', Grubby's nice little earner only came to an end with the internet in the mid-1990s. 'It was inevitable something would come along, so I wasn't that surprised. I had a long, hard think about the business and realised I needed to, shall we say, readjust my thinking.'

Ever the opportunist, Grubby then began setting up internet porn sites and sex phone-in services catering for all types of perversions. He ran his new operation from a tiny office above a jeweller's shop in the centre of Marbella's old town. 'I had three women and three men sitting there answering emails and taking calls twenty-four hours a day. It was brilliant for a couple of years.'

But Grubby still had a dream to make 'really classy porn movies' that could be broadcast over the internet. He also wanted to take full advantage of the massive influx of British residents on the Costa del Sol. 'I started approaching people with holiday homes and offering to pay them to use their houses as locations for my brand-new, slick porn movies. Then I offered to film their homes separately so that when the owners wanted to sell them they could put the footage out on the internet through local estate agents. With more and more people buying and selling properties regularly out here it worked like a dream.' Grubby says his latest business venture isn't nearly as exciting as the early days of porn, 'but I've got a steady income and I think I've been wise about moving with the times.'

Today his life revolves around occasional visits to his rented office and relaxing around the 40-feet pool of the million-pound villa he shares with his 28-year-old fourth wife Sharon. 'Look, I came here with nothing, and when I die I can't take it with me so I reckon I might as well enjoy every penny while I'm fit enough to have a good time. People get all embarrassed when I say that I make porn, but what the hell's so bad about it? You can't tell me that in every suburban street back in Britain half the men and women haven't sat down and watched a porn video. It's what makes the world go around.

PART THREE

I'M A COSTA DEL CELEBRITY, GET ME OUT OF HERE!

CHAPTER THIRTY-ONE
CELEBRITY SQUARES

Freddie Star is one of the celebs
who has found it hard to make it
work in Spain

CELEBRITY SQUARES

Along with the hundreds of thousands of Brits who've flocked onto the Costa del Sol to start a new life in recent years are a handful of celebrities. Two of the most famous are *Coronation Street* star Bev Callard and outrageous comic Freddie Starr. For some inexplicable reason, they've both chosen to live right in the middle of the vast ex-pat community where even a visit to the local supermarket is guaranteed to provoke a few comments.

Bev Callard lives behind tall iron gates in a whitewashed, red-roofed villa, which nestles among citrus trees and palms in one of the Costa del Sol's best-known resorts. When Bev upped sticks, quit the *Street* and moved to Spain in 1999, she seemed to be deliberately opting for a stress-free, pressure-free, hassle-free environment well away from the traumas of her stormy, highly publicised private life. Within months of arriving on the Costa del Sol she had adopted the kind of lifestyle that meant her biggest decision of the day was whether to take breakfast on the terrace or by the other side of the swimming pool. Back in those heady, early days in Spain, Bev said, 'Now this is what I call bliss.' With a glass of sangria in one hand she added, 'And that sort of compliment doesn't come easily for a lass from Leeds, let me tell you.'

Months earlier, Bev, then 41, husband Steve, 34, and their ten-year-old son Josh had packed all their worldy possessions into a lorry and a van and set off for their new life on the Costa del Sol. They didn't tell anyone they were leaving except their immediate neighbours in Bolton, where they lived, and a few close friends.

For almost a decade, Bev had played the role of desperate wife and manhunter Liz McDonald in *Coronation Street*. But now not even the neon lights of nearby Marbella could lure the blonde actress out of her quiet little paradise in the sun. She insisted to journalists and friends that she was going to stay put and resist all the obvious Mediterranean temptations. 'I'm happier now than at any time in my life. This is a new start for us. Some people might think it's a crazy thing to do to uproot from a comfortable home in England, but we all knew it was right for us. We have had our difficulties, Steve and I. That much is no secret. But now we have a fresh start ahead of us.'

Bev believed that her marriage problems being blasted across countless tabloids had fuelled the cracks in their relationship. Steve had been caught by the papers in a compromising relationship with another woman. There were stories about crockery being thrown and shouting matches, but Bev insisted the opposite was true. 'There was too much silence between us. We were losing the art of communicating with one another.'

As Bev settled down with husband Steve in Spain, the couple set about lovingly transforming the interior of their new home with a veritable kaleidoscope of pastel shades and an elaborate mural in the stairwell. Along the landing, Bev even had her own special 'retreat' – a room that housed her own wall-length wardrobe, mirror and a collection of 250 pairs of shoes. One corner of the downstairs office was also filled with Liz memorabilia. A scarlet stiletto shoe, set on a stone plaque, was a leaving present from the cast of the *Street*; and hanging in a frame was a tiny scrap of a black Lycra miniskirt, worn by Bev's character so often in the hit soap show.

So with Bev and her family settling down to a new start, one might have thought that the actress would continue the low profile she said she craved. Meaning every word, she explained at the time, 'The house is pretty well hidden, so we don't expect people to be climbing the walls, and we have already checked out the places we can go which the tourists will never find. Anyone has to have times when they are just allowed to be themselves. But in the main, I don't mind being a celebrity one bit. It's one part of the job. I enjoyed my years as Liz. I was so proud to be a part of the *Street*.'

But like most showbusiness stalwarts, Bev soon

started to feel the need for some attention. At her favourite restaurant, the Jamaica Inn, curious glances followed her everywhere, but the main thing was that she was being noticed...

Cut to less than a year later. Yet another tabloid headline, this one screaming, 'Bev Split with Husband Number Three', seemed to prove that the idyllic life on the Costa del Sol hadn't quite had the desired effect for Bev Callard. Add to that the fact that Bev had also returned to the *Street* as a temporary barmaid at the Rover's Return and it becomes clear that Spain isn't always the answer to all your problems.

Ironically, friends of the couple told the *Sunday Mirror* that their life in the sun was to blame for the bust-up. 'It just highlighted the cracks they had been papering over,' said one pal. But then, marriage problems were nothing new for Bev Callard. She'd first wed at 16 and had a daughter, Rebccca, who is now in her late 20s and also an actress. Marriage number two was to economics teacher David Sowden. Then along came Steve.

In the middle of all her domestic chaos in Spain, Bev set up an aerobics training school on the Costa del Sol to fill in the gaps between acting jobs. Then, in 2003, she signed for a permanent transfer back to *Coronation Street*. She'd managed to go full circle in the space of three short years.

These days she still considers her luxury home in Spain to be her main base and divides her time between there and a flat in Kilburn, north London, which is above her daughter Rebecca's flat. Today she is not so keen on discussing her private life, but she says she's very happy with her single status and her recently revived run of acting work. Son Josh is at a British boarding school and, with a second series of the TV comedy series *Two Pints of Lager and a Packet of Crisps* about to start shooting, as well as the transfer of a radio comedy show to television and talk of a starring role in a film, she is now busier than ever.

As one of Bev's closest friends says, 'She gave it all up to move to Spain and try to save her marriage. It didn't work, but then that's the mistake so many people make when it comes to the Costa del Sol. They think that a bit of sun and sangria will make everything OK, but it's the opposite. When you're stuck in a house with your husband or wife in a tricky relationship, all the problems are magnified because you haven't got your usual friends and family around you.'

It's a lesson to us all.

Freddie Starr's story is depressingly similar to Bev Callard's with one big difference: he is still living on the Costa del Sol full time. Back in 1999, Starr quit Britain claiming he had to escape the Child Support Agency after he'd been locked in battle with an ex-lover about maintenance for their three-year-old daughter. He sold his luxury home in Berkshire and his Mercedes, and bought a million-pound villa in the hills behind Torremolinos for himself and wife number three,

Donna. So it wasn't exactly a life of poverty for the comedian whose career peaked in the early-1980s when a now-notorious national newspaper headline proclaimed, 'Freddie Starr Ate my Hamster'.

By the early-1990s, he had two failed marriages behind him. Then followed a highly publicised affair with his personal assistant and a live-in relationship with a woman called Trudy Coleman, who gave birth to the child that became the focus of the maintenance row when Freddie quit Britain.

Like so many before him, Freddie Star believed that the Costa del Sol would be the answer to all his problems. He'd even blamed his very public bust-up with his child's mother Trudy as the main reason why he'd fled the UK. One of his closest friends told a journalist at the time, 'Trudy is very bitter over Freddie and will not let go of this matter. Freddie reckons she can look after herself – his main concern is Donna and their new life together in Spain. He loves the idea that he is going into tax exile.'

But life is never simple with someone as madcap as Freddie Starr, and in the summer of 2002 the Costa del Sol marriage curse struck yet again when Freddie split from Donna. Within weeks, friends were saying that the comedian was on his last legs, a lonely figure chain-smoking, chewing gum and drinking too much coffee in the lounges of hotels near his house.

Life in Spain seemed to have proved a disaster for Freddie. Instead of headline-hitting TV appearances and top-of-the-bill shows, he was now having to make do with the occasional weekend dates in Blackpool and a short, low-budget theatre tour. The divorce from 31-year-old Donna was the last straw, or so it seemed.

As Freddie himself admitted in July 2002, 'I was not ready for marriage again. I was carrying too much hurt around. We could see it wasn't working after just three months. Neither of us was capable of giving the marriage a hundred per cent.' Spain had even had the effect of making Freddie show a rarely acknowledged serious side. 'I don't give a toss. I'm giving myself another two years and then I'm retiring. Nothing is for ever.'

Now Freddie was rattling around in his large villa with only statues of Charlie Chaplin and Laurel and Hardy for company. He rarely swam in the vast pool and never sunbathed. He didn't drink and he didn't play golf. But the comedian insisted at the time, 'I'm happy living by myself. I stay in a lot of the time, working on scripts or watching sport on TV. I lead a very quiet life. I don't miss the old days when I had a £2 million mansion, owned racehorses, a helicopter and several Rolls Royces. I just look back and think, "What a dickhead!"'

But in the crazy, mixed-up world of Freddie Starr, nothing is ever as simple as it seems. Just a year after announcing his divorce from Donna the couple remarried. Freddie told one journalist, 'I can't live without her.'

He still lives in Spain, and people who have encountered him since he got back with Donna say he's a new man. 'Freddie was sinking fast just like so many older men in Spain whose marriages break up after moving here. But now they're back together he's got himself onto a TV series, he's making stand-up appearances in carefully selected local clubs and bars, and he's been out socialising again.'

But that same friend warned, 'Freddie's probably only got one more chance in life. Out here, the sun and the booze and other influences are a potent mix that so often ends in tragedy. I just hope Freddie has learned his lesson.'

CHAPTER THIRTY-TWO
PRINCE MISERABLE

Prince found himself a slave 2 the
housing market in Spain

PRINCE MISERABLE

It's the ultimate challenge for television's incredibly popular *House Doctor*. How do you make improvements to a rock superstar's house on the Costa del Sol that's so over-the-top no one wants to buy it? Answer: you make it even more vulgar by putting all the owner's personal possessions back into it.

Welcome to the extraordinary mansion that chart-topping musical eccentric Prince is so desperate to sell he's splashed out more than a million dollars to try and improve it. Now friends say it's close to rivalling Elton John's Windsor palace as the most OTT celebrity property of all time.

When superstar Prince bought this mansion on the Costa del Sol he desperately hoped it would be the key to the future happiness of himself and pretty wife Mayte. But then the couple's only child died of a rare disease just one week after birth. The stress and strain of losing their baby son soon had a devastating toll on the star's marriage. Now Prince's isolated dream home in the hills above Estepona has turned into a nightmare. He has dubbed it a 'cursed house' and vowed never to return. At one stage, the millionaire star even wanted to donate the vast property – called Adorna Tierra – to an orphanage because of the bad luck it had brought him.

The last straw came in 2003 when his views were obstructed by cranes being used to build yet more houses within a stone's throw of his once-isolated home. 'Prince went crazy, as he'd bought the house in the first place because it was so isolated; now there were cranes so high that anyone could take pictures of him in his garden,' explained local estate agent Miguel Ferrer.

Prince's difficulty in selling what his Florida-based agent rather quaintly describes as an 'English-style mansion' shows that even the richest of us can't always cash in on the worldwide property boom. Two years ago the mansion was on the market for the equivalent of €7.5 million. When it failed to sell, the diminutive superstar was persuaded to reinstall his favourite purple grand piano, splash out €200,000 on a dining-room set complete with Prince insignias and even have his personal crest painted above the swimming pool to attract buyers. And then there was the €50,000 desk in the newly decorated 'purple study', plus the return of all his most glamorous snapshots to adorn the walls, not to mention a further €100,000 worth of redecoration. He has even thrown in his beloved purple BMW, which he personally had shipped over from Georgia six years ago.

'This was all supposed to help sell the property quickly,' says one Marbella estate agent who has been watching the proceedings with bemusement. 'But it doesn't seem to have worked. Let's face it, the first thing that anyone with that kind of money will do is rip everything out and start all over again. The place looks more like a tacky furniture store in Blackpool than a classy mansion.'

To add insult to injury, Prince has even been persuaded to drop the price of the house to €5 million. 'It seems that even one of the richest rock stars on earth has had to take a terrible tumble on the property market,' added the agent.

Prince's problems began when he splashed out €3.5 million to buy the mansion seven years ago. He even had a customised basement with special soundproofing built below his office so that he could 'go down and scream his head off whenever he got stressed'. But then everything started to go wrong. 'They hardly ever went out after losing the baby. They just wanted complete privacy and that was the beginning of the end of their marriage,' explained Miguel Ferrer. 'I know that Prince has only been in the property four times in seven years for a total of three weeks. Now he hates that house and reckons it has a curse on it.'

Meanwhile, Spanish-born ex-wife Mayte occasionally drops into the mansion for holidays as lawyers continue to negotiate the financial end of the couple's four-year marriage. Prince is currently shelling out the equivalent of £15,000 a month on maintining the property and its permanent staff of five. In the past, Mayte has phoned staff at the mansion to tell them she is bringing lovers, including Tommy Lee – ex-husband of Pamela Anderson – over to Spain. Says a friend, 'Prince and Mayte have long since gone their separate ways, but Prince still considers the home to have been somewhere special for both of them and he was distressed to think she'd bring any new lovers to the property. He considered it disrespectful.'

At one stage, Tommy Lee and Mayte were said to have become 'very close' after Pamela Anderson's bad-boy ex agreed to produce an album for her in Los Angeles. The couple were even spotted openly caressing each other at an MTV party in LA. But the background to the Spanish mansion might explain why Prince was so reluctant to allow Mayte to cavort with Tommy Lee on the Costa del Sol. One Spanish associate of Prince explained, 'They bought the house with the express intention of raising a family and living happily ever after away from the bright lights of Hollywood. It's tragic that so much should go wrong for them.'

Says another local property expert, 'It's a classic scenario. The area is being overdeveloped and people are advised to try and buy the land in front of their own properties if they want to avoid such problems. It's a complete mess. Mayte loves the house because she was born in Spain, while Prince hates the place because it's surrounded by building sites and he associates it with the loss of their child.'

Prince's property representative Julisa Garcia explains to all prospective buyers that the rock superstar is so desperate to sell the house that he has set up a Spanish company to make the sale easier. From her office in Florida she tells interested parties, 'It's a fantastic house.'

As the agent's details explain, 'Adorna Tierra means ornament of earth. It is a very unique mansion that offers luxury, beauty and a lot of privacy.' The mansion also consists of a thousand square metres of garden that cost €300,000 to landscape; a personalised beauty parlour and hairdressing salon; €150,000 worth of sound, TV and video systems, including a satellite dish with 250 channels; a gym; and a guard house for a round-the-clock security man. There's also a climate-controlled Olympic-sized pool, a tennis court, the obligatory jacuzzi that fits eight people, plus a €500,000 security system, including video, cameras and radar-alarm beams across every border.

POSTSCRIPT

The Costa del Sol is a booming, thriving economy with sky-rocketing property prices accompanying a disturbing rise in crime. As thousands more Brits move into the area every month, the value of their assets rises, turning the entire area into rich pickings for ambitious criminals.

Yet the Andalusian sun will continue to shine down, the waves of the blue Mediterranean will always crash against the beautiful golden sandy beaches, and it will long continue as the ultimate dream destination for so many British residents. Where else can you still get a drinkable bottle of Rioja for around €4.50 (£3) a bottle? Television channels back in Britain provide a constant diet of 'getting away from it all' programmes that simply feed the desire to escape to the sun.

Buying a house on the Costa del Sol is now a better investment than anything back in the UK; it can also provide a lucrative additional income from a whole variety of sources, as well as the perfect retreat for any self-confessed ducker and diver. The key is some lateral thinking when it comes to putting that home to work.

It is quite remarkable how many people are prepared to fork out a small fortune to rent a 'special' holiday home.

House prices have tripled in the past five years; that's faster than anywhere else in mainland Europe. Even on those Brookside-style estates with identical houses that have swamped the areas behind the overcrowded tourist hotspots like Marbella, Estepona and Fuengirola, a relatively modest three-bedroom house can set you back £300,000.

Demand for luxurious properties on the edge of the Mediterranean is booming as never before, partly thanks to the strength of the pound against the euro. Alcohol, food and petrol remain cheaper in mainland Spain, and even the local health service is a lot more impressive than anything on offer back in the UK.

Some have plumped for buying a *finca* in the hills behind the Costa del Sol. There are now so many Brits in these areas that it has become known as the Cotswolds of Spain. The trouble is that most end up sweating blood and tears before getting their properties fully renovated, often by greedy rip-off builders who usually turn out to be unscrupulous fellow Brits. The last family I knew who did this are still waiting to move into their dream holiday home four years after buying it.

Most houses on the Costa del Sol are no more than one hour's drive from Malaga Airport, and the motorways of southern Spain are wonderfully empty of vehicles once you get out of the big cities. They are so new that a lot of the locals still prefer sticking to the more familiar B roads. Malaga has more flights to and from the UK than any other city in Europe. These days many people buy one-way tickets at short notice from bucket shops at Malaga Airport. Even standbys work if you're travelling alone or in a pair. One can fly to or from Malaga for as little as £20 – less than the cost of a rail ticket from London to Brighton.

So the cold, hard reality is that the Costa del Crime will continue to grow. 'It would take a world war to slow down development here,' says one who should know. But perhaps those who have been tempted to set up home here will now have a more realistic idea of what to expect.

APPENDIX 1

Some of the high-profile murders of Britons on the Costa del Crime in recent years

Gangland enforcer Scott Bradfield, 28: battered to death, cut up and stuffed into two trunks near Torremolinos in November 2001. His body was left in an exposed position as a warning to other criminals on the Costa del Sol.

Northern Ireland-born Michael McGuinness, 36: found bound and gagged in the boot of his car in Malaga in August 2000. He had earlier been kidnapped at gunpoint from his apartment in Mijas on the Costa del Sol.

Retired British businessman Eric Robinson: killed by a drug-addict burglar at his home near Marbella in January 2000.

British estate agent Irene Mulvihill: found murdered in June 2001 in the garden of her £300,000 home in Mijas, where she lived with her husband and daughter.

Tourist Richard Winter: battered to death with a hammer on the marble floor of his Torremolinos apartment in November 1997.

Robin Lewis, 43, originally from Enfield, Middlesex: shot and then set alight at the side of a motorway on the Costa del Sol in April 1997. Police believe Lewis had double-crossed a Columbian drug cartel.

Tory councillor's musician daughter Susan Kendrick, 32: found dead in a remote ravine near Estepona in October 1995. She had been sexually assaulted.

Gerald McDonald: killed when gunmen shot a hail of bullets into a pub in Fuengirola in July 1996. Three others were injured.

Bar owner George Hansford: murdered and mutilated before being chopped into five pieces at his villa on the Costa del Sol in February 1995.

Wife of businessman Jeremy Lowndes: beaten to death by her husband at their Costa del Sol villa. Lowndes was jailed for nine years in June 1994.

APPENDIX 2

Fifty things you probably never knew about the Costa del Crime

1 Half a million British tourists visit the Costa del Sol each summer.
2 250,000 Brits now live on the Costa del Sol.
3 Of those 250,000, substantially more than half are men.
4 There are estimated to be more than a hundred brothels in the Malaga province.
5 There are a total of 25,000 bars and nightclubs on the Costa del Sol.
6 There are 300 beaches.
7 In 2003, more than 500 people were arrested by Spanish police for having sex on beaches.
8 It is estimated that, out of the 150,000 single Brits travelling to the Costa del Sol each year, more than 10,000 will come back with sexually transmitted diseases.
9 More than 350,000 Germans will also visit this summer.

10 At least 30 contract killings are carried out in the province of Malaga each year.

11 Drug barons finance legitimate business in the Costa del Sol to the tune of half a billion pounds each year.

12 More than 100,000 golfers visit the Costa del Sol each year.

13 There are more than 50 golf courses on the coast.

14 There are more than 20,000 hotels.

15 Puerto Banus has more hookers than any other resort, with an estimated 2,000 working girls.

16 The city of Malaga provides the cheapest sex, with rates as low as £30 for 30 minutes.

17 One Marbella private-investigations agency specialises in sending hookers in to 'test' husbands suspected of adultery by their wives.

18 Fuengirola and Torremolinos are estimated to contain a total of 35,000 gay British men and women.

19 British golfers are the most generous tippers at the strip clubs of Puerto Banus.

20 Benalmadena has the lowest-per-capita income Brits on the coast.

21 The latest craze at one Estepona golf course is naked play.

22 More Guinness is consumed on the Costa del Sol than in the whole of London.

23 Spanish residents on the Costa del Sol make up less than half the total population.

24 It is estimated that a total of 10,000 women on the

than anywhere else than Los Angeles.

38 More Viagra is sold per head of population on the Costa del Sol than anywhere else in Europe.

39 French and German naturists make up more than 70 per cent of all the nudists who visit the Costa del Sol.

40 Hookers spend an estimated £100,000 each month advertising their services in local newspapers and on the internet.

41 One legendary Marbella hooker called Candice claims to have serviced 30 men and 10 women in one day.

42 More than 35 per cent of all the female hookers on the Costa del Sol are gay.

43 The Costa's 50 sex shops earn more than £1 million per month.

44 Hookers in the luxury resort of Puerto Banus make an average of €4,500 a week.

45 Hundreds of hookers arrive on the Costa del Sol every month looking for work.

46 More than 50 per cent of all hookers here are married or in long-term relationships.

47 There are more than a thousand pimps working alongside hookers on the Costa del Sol.

48 At least two Brits die in brothels every month from heart attacks.

49 Twenty per cent of all female hookers on the Costa del Sol are Brits.

50 The divorce rate on the Costa del Sol is one of the highest in Europe.

coast work as part-time hookers to supplement their income.

25 STD clinics along the Costa del Sol are filled to bursting point throughout the busy summer months.

26 There are estimated to be more than 5,000 swingers – mainly British, German and Spanish – on the Costa del Sol.

27 More internet sex lines are operated here than from any other area in Europe.

28 At least 200 men and women couples work as joint hookers offering voyeurs the chance to watch them have sex for £100 per hour.

29 There were at least 5,000 breast-implant operations carried out at clinics on the Costa del Sol last year.

30 And at least 2,500 penis implants.

31 More than a hundred sex dungeons exist on the Costa del Sol.

32 Spanish porn videos are said to be the most explicit in Europe thanks to relaxed local laws.

33 The fastest-growing sex market on the Costa del Sol is for handsome single men to service businesswomen.

34 The sex industry here is said to employ a total of 40,000 people.

35 There are more blonde women under the age of 30 on the Costa del Sol than in any other area of Europe.

36 The area has an average of more than 300 days of sunshine every year.

37 There are more Rolls Royces on the Costa del Sol